The Basics of Consulting Process

The way to understand, design, and lead the changes

JW Seol & Dr. Minho Cho

DEDICATION

To our loving family and our kids who will make our
aspirations come true.

Yongsoo, Aran, Craig Min, Brian Kyung

CONTENTS

Consulting starts with problem solving and ends with change management.

"Americans have a tendency to believe that when
there's a problem there must be a solution."
— Henry Kissinger (1923 ~), Former United States
Secretary of State

聲不過五, 五聲之變, 不可勝聽也. 色不過五, 五色之變, 不可勝觀也.
味不過五, 五味之變, 不可勝嘗也. (孫子), BC544? – BC496?

"There are not more than five musical notes, yet the
combinations of these five give rise to more melodies than
can ever be heard. There are not more than five primary
colors, yet in combination they produce more hues than can
ever been seen. There are not more than five cardinal tastes,
yet combinations of them yield more flavors than can ever be
tasted." — Sun Tzu (BC544? – BC496?), The Art of War

"People don't resist change. They resist being changed!"

– **Peter Senge**, the founding chair of SoL (Society of Organizational
Learning), Senior Lecturer, Sloan School of Management MIT

ACKNOWLEDGMENTS

Practice makes perfect.

Humanity has gone through a process of organizing knowledge and skills through planning, problem solving, execution, experience and learning. Along the way, there were uncertainties about various causes, workarounds, and performance, and humanity tried to choose the best method in a given situation and limited knowledge. At times, fundamental changes and changes were necessary to the existing order and system, and we began to ponder how to manage the backlash and resistance to change. As such, it can be said that consulting has made history together in all decision-making and execution processes of organizations and industrial activities.

With technology improvement and engineering of business operation, consulting service is becoming more diverse and complex. Compared to the past, the consulting field is expanding, work is more complex, and execution is more important than planning. For example, online business models existed conceptually in 30 years ago, but it was impossible to navigate the market and competition. In the same vein, globalization and multinational corporations have existed for a long time, but global supply chains have been difficult to implement. Also, using information and communication technology to transfer services to low-cost countries remained at the level of an idea.

In the past, business process innovation was a high-risk mid- to long-term task, such as changing the engine of a flying airplane. Recent business innovations are oriented toward continuous implementation through rapid implementation and verification by field. The competitive environment also focused on positioning within the market and the competitive environment between suppliers, but now it is becoming more important to establish a new competitive environment with the market and consumer-led value chain reorganization.

This book deals with the entire process-oriented process in order to acquire and internalize the core competencies necessary to solve the consulting work required in a complex business environment. We cited materials from previously published books, and reflected feedback from readers through lectures so that even those who are new to consulting can understand the content easily.

We have delivered various topics of consulting projects as an independent consultants or internal advisory in the fields of manufacturing, financial services, digital business model, and IT services industries since the 1990s. This book is prepared to help clients who need consulting and those who want to become consultants by organizing their experiences and knowledge.

Over our experiences in the various industries of different countries such as Korea, the United States, and India, there was no client with the same problem or competitive environment. Also, there was no task that could be applied the readymade solution. It was a painful moment to define the problem, develop a solution, and persuade them to get support and implement it. Nevertheless, we frankly admit that not all consulting projects have been groundbreaking and completed successfully.

This book prides itself on being faithful to providing a basic framework that can be commonly understood and utilized not only by those who start consulting, but also by customers who want to receive consulting.

JW Seol & Dr. Minho Cho

References)
Minho Cho, Jeung Seol, Consulting Process, Korea, 1999
Jeung Seol, Minho Cho, Consulting Practice, Korea, 2002
Minho Cho, Jeung Seol, Introduction to Consulting, Korea, 2006

THE BASICS OF CONSULTING PROCESS

CHAPTER 1. OVERVIEW

1.1 Introduction

Definition of Consulting

Just as a doctor treats a patient and provides a prescription, a consultant analyzes a company and takes measures as necessary. For instance, a patient goes to a hospital for health prevention, visits a hospital for treatment, takes medications to relieve physical and mental pain, and discovers and prepares for anticipated symptoms through a health check-up. Similarly, companies and organizations ask an independent consultancy for diagnosis and find a remedy to resolve the issues when they face business challenges comparing expectations.

"Management consulting is an independent professional advisory service assisting managers and organizations in achieving organizational purposes and objectives by solving management and business problems, identifying and seizing new opportunities, enhancing learning and implementing changes." ILO (International Labor Organization)[1]

---

[1] Management Consulting. A guide to the profession, 4th ed, 2002

Key Features of Consulting

We can identify five key characteristics of consulting as follows.

- Professional services

  - It delivers solutions under the defined root causes with observations upon the professional knowledge of subject matter experts. It is highly required to keep ethical compliance maintaining to protect client's interest.

- Advisory services

  - The final deliverables may be applied to business decisions. However, it should be limited to advising a solution for a final decision maker. Consultancy does not have the authority to decide on behalf of the client and cannot drive implementation without the client's approval. Consultancy services are responsible to deliver a quality deliverable that contains the most effective and practical solutions under given conditions.

THE BASICS OF CONSULTING PROCESS

- Independent services

    - It is critically important to make a report with an independent point of view regardless of the relationship with the client.
    - Recommendations should not intentionally give favor to a specific service provider or product. Also, it is not an independent service if the deliverables state a solution to make a recurring business from the client. At the same time, the report needs to keep an independent position against the internal politics of the client. Such an internal consultancy will be hard to keep an independent position under certain circumstances. However, an internal consultant also needs to justify and deliver a deliverable under in-depth assessment-based facts.

- Temporary services

    - It is not a permanent service to provide consultancy for clients. A consultant is usually asked to engage when the client does not have enough capability or available resources. Once the consultant delivers the services and achieves the objectives of consulting, it needs to be forwarded to the client for ongoing operation with internalization. In certain cases, a client may want to maintain internal consultancy however, internal consultancy is also reorganized according to the objectives in a regular manner.

- Commercial services

    - The consultancy provides a professional service, and the client is responsible to pay the agreed contract value. The scope, deliverables, and payment schedule of consulting services will be defined on the mutually agreed service contract.

What we want to achieve through consulting

- Achieve goals

    - All the consultancy services pursue to accomplish business and organizational priorities. Leadership design, product portfolio, quality management, production optimization, pricing scheme, profitability assessment, competency review, and business transformation may be an example of the priorities. It will have a bit different perspective for the same priority. For instance, private companies look for profitability to improve shareholder value. However, a non-profit organization may be looking for profitability to minimize taxpayers' burden-sharing.

    - Despite the different perspectives for priorities of

what the client wants to get thru consulting, one common purpose of consulting service is to pursue tangible and measurable contributions accomplishing the objective of consulting what the client suggested. Some clients may not have identified or internally agreed with objectives to get accomplished while they get consultancy services. For this case, the consultant initiatives a project to review and develop scope with the purpose of the consulting project.

- Problem solving

  - The most generally known purpose of consulting is to help client makes a decision to solve problems. It begins with identifying problems and defining a root cause to discover a solution. Problem[2] tells gaps between expectations and the current state that the client faces today. In other words, a problem is the same as gaps comparing targets and challenges against reality. While the consultant defines a problem, it is recommended to interpret the current state and expectations with more holistic perspectives. If the problem is identified with a specific position or interest, it will not bring the correct framework to do it right and stick to finding a stop-gap solution instead of a radical

---

[2] Expectation may be classified by several points such as 1) Aspiration to accomplish goals, 2) Run business as usual to provide a return as expected, 3) Improve the business process to meet legal/compliance.

resolution.

- Discover and develop new opportunity

    - The consultant's responsibilities are not limited to solving current problems but developing new business opportunities. Many companies are looking for an opportunity to take market leadership, improve business processes, penetrate the market, improve quality, enhance customer satisfaction, motivate employees' competency, enhance shareholder value, etc.

- Learning organization

    - Management leadership of client expects to see their organization learns and grows by getting consultants' knowledge with experience. Group learning promotes improving organizational competencies and building organizational foundations to transform business later.

- Implement change

    - "Change agent" is another name for a consultant. It is necessary to drive and promote the change across the organization in every step when implementing opportunities upon consulting deliverables. As a change agent, the consultant helps a client understand why change for what for now and brings them into the journey of change heading for transformation.

Besides, the client looks for consultancy services when they need to get below.

- External advice beyond internal politics
- Spin-off business and initiate new business with high risk
- Temporarily requires a group of highly trained resources

1.2 History of consulting

Before industrial revolution

In general, consulting has various kinds of definitions by domain since human beings had civilized. Some say that the first consulting in history begins with the advice given in the Bible Genesis. It is said that God's words to Adam and Eve, "Do not eat of the forbidden fruit," were the first advice in the prehistoric age. In the started bronze age, human beings had formed a tribal society most of them working in the agricultural industry. As a leader of tribal society, a chieftain had to forecast weather, and allocate their resources for farming. Also, the prophecy against natural disasters and tribal warfare was always a priority to deal with as a chieftain.

The method that relied on intuitive or subjective judgment needed a philosophy for more systematic governance and a strategy to preoccupy the superiority of power among countries as the country emerged. In B.C. Socrates, Plato, Aristotle, and others suggested philosophical thinking. In the Middle Ages, Thomas Aquinas, Confucius, Zhuge Liang, and others suggested a religious worldview, government management, and military strategies for victory in war.

Industrial revolution: Early stage of consulting

In the industrial age, a more scientific approach had applied to business operations. Division of labor and motion study to improve productivity was a dominant trend, it had been deployed to most business functions. Below tells several key trends in the 20th century.

- The advent of scientific management
    - Charles T. Sampson, 1870
    - Redesigned the assembly process of shoe factory for an unskilled worker, the knowledge with experience has transferred to his next door.

- Deployment of scientific management
    - Frederick W. Taylor, Frank and Lillian Gilbreth, Henry L. Gantt, Harrington Emerson
    - Simplify work processes and improve productivity.
    - Consulting through lectures, research, writing textbooks and articles

- Structural approach for business management
    - Edwin Booz, 1914, Business Research Services
    - In the 1920s, actively researched human resource management through Elton Mayo's Hawthorne test.
    - 1925, James O. McKinsey, analytical approaches to business management

Postwar, the golden age of consulting

Consulting played a significant role in the efficient operation of the military and national management for the victory of World War II. In particular, new technologies such as Operation Research for efficient material procurement were initially applied for military purposes but gradually came to be used for business and public purposes. From the Second World War to 1980, the demand for consulting expanded significantly according to the rapid technological change, the development project management of the new economy, and the rapidly increasing internationalization of the world's industry, commerce, and finance.

Also, information technology has played a key role as an enabler for factory automation, employee communications, quality management, facility management, software development project management, market research, and compliance. At the same time, the global operation model, cross-border supply chain, and governance are getting more interest from multi-national companies.

In other cases, there are recently emerging trends appeared that many clients want to utilize consultancy when they create or build a new business model. Comparing the typical agenda of consulting services, shaping a new business model requires completely different competencies which are rarely maintained by the client's internal organization. It requires multi factors of capabilities such as market intelligence, strategy, regulatory, talent acquisition, design entity structure, funding, and exit strategy.

Contemporary topics of consulting services

Historically, consulting service has started in the manufacturing industry to improve productivity upon statistical analysis and deployed to other functions such as finance, accounting, and other business functions. Since the 1970s, with the development project management of information technology, information technology has been regarded as an enabler to build common business platform and plays a key role as a catalyst in developing business opportunities and bringing new sources of income.[3]

- Strategy

    - Mid-to-long-term strategy, Program management
    - Global operation
    - Business spin-off, Alliance
    - Governance, Social responsibility

- Production

---

[3] https://www.consultancy.org/consulting-industry

- Productivity, Value engineering
- Process design, Quality control
- Production footprint
- Product mix optimization
- Smart manufacturing

- Human resources

  - Human resource development, Retention,
  - Compensation, Talent management

- Finance

  - Profitability improvement
  - Asset valuation, Cost rationalization, IFRS[4], Financing strategy

- Procurement

  - Inventory management, Logistics, Global logistics, Sourcing strategy,

- Market Intimacy

  - Market penetration
  - Sales channel consolidation

---

[4] IFRS, International Financial Reporting Standards

- Pricing optimization
- Sales program, Standard and regulation
- Trade compliance, Investor relationship

- **Information Technology**

  - IT strategy planning, IT capability assessment
  - IT organization and governance
  - IT service quality management, IT service operation, Service desk, IT procurement
  - Database optimization
  - Cloud strategy, DevOps
  - Standard, policy, and principle
  - IT security
  - Intrusion detection and prevention

- **Technology**

  - Technology adoption, deployment, and migration
  - New products development
  - Intellectual Property

- **Business convergence**

  - Business modeling
  - Digital transformation, Open innovation, Design thinking

1.3 Qualifying Consultant

Who is a consultant?

A consultant provides advice and guidance with professional insight on the management challenges of a company or organization. Although the definition of a consultant will be varied depending on the point of view, we will introduce some representative ones in this section.

A consultant is a person who understands the nature of business problems through a thorough analysis based on facts from the perspective of the top management, suggests the optimal solution for the client's situation, and continuously supports the client for effective implementation of the solution. [McKinsey & Company]

A consultant is a person with an excellent education, experience, and technical skills necessary to identify issues specific to management, including the organization, planning, direction, control, and operation of an enterprise, and to support them in a professional position to solve problems, providing impartial and objective advice a person who serves a company. [ACME[5]]

A consultant is an expert from outside the company who

---

[5] Association of Management Consulting Firms, http://www.amcf.org/

provides support for rationalization and advancement of corporate management in terms of rationalization and advancement of corporate management, conducting various activities such as pointing out management problems, suggesting improvement, guidance on the implementation of improvement plans, and education for the overall corporate management or each sector. [Japanese Ministry of Trade, Industry, and Energy]

Roles and responsibilities of consultant

- Fact-based analysis
- Diagnose problems and discover solutions
- Develop opportunities and solutions
- Draft an implementation plan
- Provide operating system
- Drive organizational change
- Train and develop talent
- Advisory and counseling
- Objective and independent justification
- Out-of-box thinking
- Domain expertise
- Communication and facilitation
- Change management
- Deploy new system

Required professional competency as a consultant

The knowledge that a consultant needs can be broadly classified into four categories.

- Ground skill
    - Communication, Counselling
    - Research, Education
    - Presentation, Facilitation, Interview
    - Survey, Statistical analysis
    - Problem-solving and execution
    - Logical thinking
    - Networking

- Business acumen
    - Domain knowledge for each business function
    - Analysis and diagnosis

- Project management
    - Issue management
    - Change management
    - Project planning and proposal
    - Program management
    - Risk management

The personal capabilities of a consultant can be divided into natural abilities and nurtured abilities. Natural abilities include intellectual and physical abilities. Nurtured abilities include people management, issue management, problem-solving, leadership, passion, spirit, and communication.

The most important capabilities as consultants expected from clients and consultants are analytical skills, creativity, and integrity. Besides these foundation capabilities, a consultant is to expect additional capabilities such as positive thinking, teamwork, devotion, commitment, and professional attitudes. When a consultant delivers a report, a client usually expects to get independent advice based on rationale with fact analysis. At the same time, a consultant is asked to keep a fiduciary duty maintained when they deal with subjective interests.

Common features of successful consultants

- Persuasive justification
- Confidence
- Flexibility
- Problem solver
- Creativity
- Self-motivation
- Trustworthy
- Interpersonal skill
- Integrity
- Diligent

Usually, a client faces passive or negative responses from stakeholders while driving changes. The most critical capability as a consultant will be execution. However, it does not mean that consultant needs to lead the implementation of action items with ownership. It does mean that consultant needs to motivate and encourage changes with action items under priorities.

1.4 Career development

As a consultant, career development will be an ongoing interest to keep improving capabilities for the next level position. Although a consultant has trained as a problem solver, specialist, conductor, and counselor for a client, they need to develop themselves like other professional experts.

What does the career path of a consultant look like? It may be different by domain or industry. If the industry has a common standard[6] or policy, a certificate or license is an example of qualifications to begin a career as a consultant. In a process-driven domain, logical thinking, facilitation, and problem-solving skills will be important competencies compared to experience. For instance, process-driven consulting deals with root causes and idea generation. It requires more multi-dimensional analysis and validation techniques. In other cases, industry consulting requires experiences better than logical thinking itself. If a client expects to get a consulting service for quality improvement in the assembly line, an experienced subject matter expert who has statistical competency should fit the expectation.

Also, the consulting domain may require another specific competency as a foundation skillset. Advertising and marketing campaign requires market intimacy. A consultant usually depends on a survey or focus group interview to understand

---

[6] For instance, ISO 2000, GAAP, Trade compliance, etc.

market dynamics, and statistical analysis capability is mandatory knowledge to start a junior consultant.

In another case, database optimization is an ongoing priority when a data architect maintains the existing services or builds a new one. To review the database scheme and improve its performance, a consultant should have knowledge about data relationships, transaction volume, historical data, and even hardware architecture. As a junior consultant, it cannot deliver the services as those required capabilities are not able to get trained at the entry point.

Regardless of their consulting domains or industry, the career development paths are similar as below.

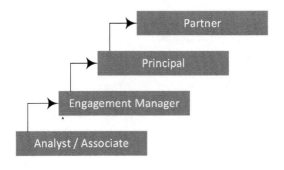

- Analysts / Associate

    - Analysts or associate does not have the authority to decide or direct the objective of a consulting project. However, they do the majority of the actual analysis and own individual work streams. According to the task of each project plan, they conduct industry research and interviews. They build an analytics model in a spreadsheet, data collection, and draft presentation slides on the key insights.

- Under the given assignment, analysts and associates are expected to work independently with minimal oversight to get the job done.

- **Engagement Managers**

  - Engagement manager spends their time structuring a problem, clarifying root causes, verifying findings, and managing the deliverables. So, their major responsibility is to ensure that analysts are on track, aren't blocked on any given analysis, and are getting the necessary support or training from him/herself.

  - They review, adjust, refine, and synthesize the deliverables of each work stream. Also, they share progress updates with the senior team leaders to get them validated before delivering to the client. Lastly, managers will also spend some time directly interacting with the client, depending on factors such as the severity of a key concern raised by the client by phase.

- **Principal**

- Principal is usually called a partner in training. This is great but tough for a principal. It is a great responsibility because they are tightly working with the top management of a client. But it is a tough assignment because they are asked to prove that they have the capabilities to drive the project under defined time and resources. Also, they have to encourage changes and manage resistance on behalf of a client. Internally, a principal has to show capabilities that they can develop new business from clients.
- Their primary responsibilities are addressing the stakeholders of a client in a day-to-day manner, managing the mid-level consultants, and keeping the partners abreast of the project status such as key findings, milestones, and any potential blockers.

- Partner

  - They cultivate new business opportunities for the firm and manage the relationship with the existing client. It does mean that the role is split between sales efforts to get a new project and deliver the existing project as they've committed.
  - Typically, they address the top management of a client directly while the team conducts a project and get their insight to reflect on the direction. For making a new project, a partner does have an initial meeting with a prospective client and supports them to refine their scope with

expectation. If necessary, a partner decides to mobilize an internal team for initial review and help a client prepare a request for proposal.

1.5 Consulting service organization

A consulting firm organizes consultants with the unit called practices or sector to deliver services. The practice or sector is classified by services, industry, and geography although project resource is mobilized across services and geography.

The consulting firm faces challenges to make sure quality services and maintain talent consistently. A quality report is generated by well-trained and experienced consultants; however, it is not practically easy to acquire and maintain talent all time due to market demand, talent shortage, and compensation schemes. For instance, trade compliance is a critically required service when a client designs and implement a global supply chain, but it does not have demand all year round in all industry. In other cases, organizational change management is a quite important practice to transform business operations however, it is more likely a long journey that requires more than a year and it is not easy to assess the accomplishment of consulting services in a short-term window.

As a result, many consulting firms aim at a lean and agile operation model nevertheless of their business size. At the same time, resource utilization is one of the measures to assess the business healthy of a consulting firm, profitability instead of sales volume is also a key metric of the consulting services. To run the organization in agile, consulting services organization typically has a flat structure with a minimum portion of supporting overhead staff such as employees in finance and human resources.

Because a consulting firm has to balance the development of specific knowledge areas with the focus on selling to and delivering services to clients in a specific area or industry upon demand, most firms select a matrix organizational structure.

Management Hierarchy

For a consultant position, it has usually five to six bands such as business analyst, consultant, senior consultant, engagement manager, associate partner, and managing partner based on capabilities with experience. Many consulting firms have an "up or out" policy where if you're not promoted to the next role after a certain number of years, likely you'll never be promoted.

Practice Areas

Consulting firms provide advice to clients in specific practice areas. The practice area is set up based on industry as well as functional area which is aligned with market demand. Each practice typically has a global or national practice leader and might have regional or local practice leaders, depending on the size of the firm. Most consulting projects deliver the services by practice areas, but sometimes collaboration across practice areas is required when a client asks for changes across the organization.

Geographic Focus

If consulting organization delivers shared services operation to a multi-national company, they may have the services organized by region by function. In case of standardized service, it tends to consolidate the services instead of maintaining the services in every region. 24 x 7 call center has a similar operation model, and they provide the services following the sun. Also, underwriting, billing & collection, and credit review services are also generally consolidated by region instead of running the services by state.

Matrix Structure

Usually, it is not able to deliver the services by one practice area as consulting organization prefers to keep efficiencies in an agile manner. Also, client expects to get the advisory with industry expertise as well as functionalities point of view. For instance, sourcing strategy in the discrete manufacturing industry requires industry domain knowledge as well as process expertise. Matrix organization works perfectly for these demands. At the beginning of project, industry experts discover business challenges with desired states, and functional consultant redesign the process under an aligned direction. For the matrix structure, each organization maintains a different measure to assess consultant's accomplishment. If industry practice gets performance review based on contract value, functional practice may get the assessment according to resources utilization or contribution margin for the intracompany transaction.

1.6 Academic foundation of consulting process

Lewin three step model (1947)

Lewin has classified three steps[7] to lead a successful change project as below[8].

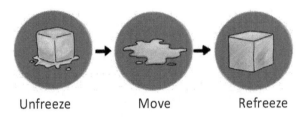

Unfreeze   Move   Refreeze

- Unfreezing

    - The first step of accepting that change is necessary. Therefore, break down the current organizational structure and start from the core to build a new structure. This enables organizations to reevaluate their processes. Promote motivation to increase acceptance across the organization for an upcoming change.

---

[7] Kurt Lewin, "Group Decision and Social Change", 1947
[8] Image source, https://practicalpie.com/lewins-change-theory

- Moving

    - The phase of resolving the issue identify by unfreeze stage.
    - Transition from previous methods to new environment.
    - Implement the change under priority
    - Deploy new process and system into existing model
    Transform operations.

- Refreezing

    - The part where organization ensures successful implementation of change.
    - Stabilize and make it concrete once the change is implemented.

Magerison's 12-Step Consulting Model (1986)

Lastly, let's have an opportunity to introduce the Magerison model, which is not widely applied but suggested from an academic point of view. What is called 12 steps[9] provides a

---

[9] Charles J. Margerison, "Consulting Activities in Organisational Change",

basis for assessing any advisory project. Although they are written in sequential order, the real-life consulting project does not always fall easily into such a pattern. To study what we do identify at any point in time where we are, the 12 steps provide a practical solution for a consultant. It has three stages such like appraisal, assessment, and application and each stage has four steps respectively.

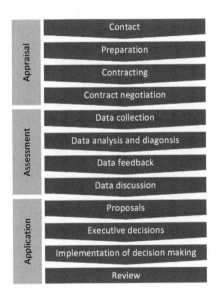

- Appraisal

    Contact

Journal of Organizational Change Management, 1988

- This is the initial meeting to discuss the problem or opportunity. You are approached, or you make the contact, and discuss a broad overview of the issues with an agreement usually to meet again, if you pick up the main cues and the client recognizes your willingness and ability to help.

Preparation
- This is the thinking and preparation time when you may send your initial thoughts to the client's end, if they agree, you have a meeting for an in-depth discussion of the presenting symptoms. It is here that you begin to get to know the actors and their scripts.

Contracting
- This is an outline proposal of what could be done, by whom, when, where, how, why, and at what cost. The details are usually written down and sent as a proposal letter after the contracting discussion.

Contract Negotiation
- This is where you negotiate details of the contract. The client assesses the proposal and discusses it with the relevant people before agreeing or proposing amendments agreeing with the terms.

- Assessment

  Data Collection
  - Assuming a contract is agreed upon, you proceed to gather relevant data through interviews, group meetings, questionnaires, or whatever is the appropriate approach.

  Data Analysis and Diagnosis
  - Opportunity to assess the data and review how it should be used with the client, and the set-up of the organizational and meeting arrangements.

  Data Feedback
  - The presentation of the data, either orally or by written report or a combination thereof, then takes place.

  Data Discussion
  - There follows the discussion of the issues in terms of the objectives and purposes. This is usually best done with the consultant present to clarify points arising and avoid misunderstanding.

- Application

  Proposals
  - The data feedback at step 7 may or may not have contained a proposal. However, proposals will, or at least should, emerge from the discussion of the data. If possible, it is usually best to discuss the data and clarify its meaning separately from discussing proposals for action. The proposal stage is a vital one and should involve considerable concentration on options and opportunities using every creative idea available.

  Executive Decisions
  - The client, individually or collectively, comes to decisions based on the data discussion with or without any advice from you. Ultimately, it must be their decision otherwise, you will end up managing their business.

  Implementation of decision making
  - This is an executive function that from time to time they may want to delegate to you or others. However, a vital aspect of consulting is advising on implementation otherwise, the early steps may be wasted. Beware of crossing the thin line between proposing and doing unless you have, by agreement, taken on the latter role.

Review
-   An assessment of how the assignment has gone both objectively. In terms of factual results, as well as subjectively, in terms of people's feelings, should take place to learn from the intervention.

Kolb & Frohman., The process of planned change (1970)

They've published an article in 1970 to structure the process leading to planned changes, and it is valuable theory to form consulting process in later. The article has described several key features of each step and cited the original statement below[10] to get correct insights. Although it has been 50+ years since they have published, it gives a logical skeleton to consulting process.

---

[10] David A Kolb, Alan L Frohman., "Organizational develop project management through planned change: a develop project management model", Massachusetts Institute of Technology, 1970

THE BASICS OF CONSULTING PROCESS

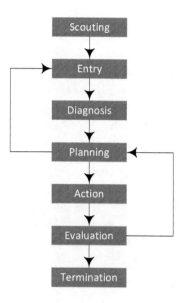

- Scouting

    - "The critical goal of this phase is for the consultant to identify the best point for him to enter the system he is trying to change. In addition, it is at this point that the consultant is "scouting" his interests, values, and priorities to decide whether this client system is one with which he wants to work.... The first scouting goal is often to answer the question, "What about their perception of me and their problem led them to contact me?"

- Entry

    - "Once the entry point has been chosen, the consultant and client system through the entry point representative begin to negotiate a "contract". The "contract" will define if and how the succeeding stages of the planned change process will be carried out. "Contract" is used here in quotation marks because this process implies more than a legal document agreed upon at the outset of a project. The emphasis here is much more on a continuing process of sharing the expectations of the consultant and client system and agreeing on the contributions to be made by both parties."

- Diagnosis

    - "The main object of the diagnostic phase is to move toward the improvement of client system functioning by changing vaguely felt difficulties into specific problems. Diagnosis focuses on four elements: the client's felt problem, the client system's goals, and client and consultant resources. The starting point for the diagnosis is the client's felt problem. Beginning with the client's sense of the problem facilitates the meeting of the client's needs and his involvement and interest in the diagnostic phase. If more and/or different problems are identified as the diagnosis progresses, the client and consultant can assign priorities and focus attention on the most important problem or the problem which must be solved before other problems can be attacked."

- Planning

    - "The first planning step is to define the objectives to be achieved by the change. Once clear-cut objectives have been established, alternative solutions or change strategies can be generated. Following this, some attempt should be made to simulate the consequences of each of the alternatives. Often this is done simply by "thinking through" the implications of each change strategy; but more sophisticated simulation methods such as computer simulation can be used. The final change strategy is then chosen from the alternatives available. The simulation can also be useful in selecting criteria by which the change can be evaluated. It is important that interim as well as long term means of monitoring the change be built into the action plan. It is necessary to evaluate the progress of the change and use as a reinforcement of change to the client."

- Action

    - "If the work of the previous four phases has been done well the action plan should proceed smoothly. If there are hitches or problems these can usually be traced to unresolved issues in the early phases. If these errors are not so great as to disrupt the total change effort, they can become useful "critical incidents" for learning more about the client system. Action interventions can be classified on two dimensions - the source of power used to implement the intervention and the organizational subsystem to which the intervention is addressed."

- Evaluation

  - "The evaluation of the change strategy is conducted in terms of the objectives defined during the planning phase. It is usually useful to evaluate the change against task subgoals which will indicate if the change is progressing as desired. The client should be able to monitor the progress of the action and evaluate the data. This decreases the dependency on the consultant and develops within the client system the ability to use the information generated within the system for self-analysis.
  - It also is essential to allow the client the self-control and self-direction necessary for independence. The results of the evaluation stage determine whether the change project moves to the termination stage or returns to the planning stage for further action planning and perhaps further contract negotiation with the client." The tradition in the scientific evaluation of change projects has been to separate the evaluation phase from the

action phase.

- In many cases, an independent researcher is hired to evaluate the change efforts so that the results will not be biased. ... Criteria for evaluation are defined in terms of the objectives set forth in the planning phase." Evaluate how far objectives have been achieved and decide whether to continue or discontinue.

- **Termination**

  - "... Most consulting relationships are conceived to bring about some improvement in the client system's functioning that will continue after the consultant leaves. Because of these characteristics of the consulting relationship, the issue of termination must be given attention throughout the relationship from beginning to end. In the initial entry contract, the conditions of termination should be discussed and tentatively agreed upon. ... There are two different termination situations - success and failure. Success has two aspects: 1) achievement of the goals outlined in the entry-diagnosis-planning phases and 2) improvement of the client system's ability to achieve similar goals in the future. While in the success case the termination point is often quite clear, the problem of client dependence can often cloud the issue."

McKinsey 7-step Problem-solving Process (1996)[11]

Define Problem — Think Impact:
What does the client need to know?

Structure Problem — Think disaggregation & early hypothesis:
What could be key elements of the prblem?

Prioritize Issues — Think speed:
Which issues are most important?

Plan Analysis and Work — Think Efficiency:
Where and how should the team spend its time?

Conduct Analysis — Think Evidence:
What are we trying to prove/disprove?

Synthesize Findings — Think "So What":
What implications do our findings have for the client?

Develop Recommendation — Think Potential Solution:
What should the client do?

We can see several frameworks of problem-solving procedures that start with defining a problem, developing a solution, and ending by selecting the solution upon evaluation. Compared with other methodologies, McKinsey suggests a highlighted step for defining the problem to get it right first.

---

[11] "The McKinsey Approach to Problem Solving", McKinsey Staff Paper, No.66, Jul.2007

The most powerful thing is to step back and ask the basic questions[12]—"What are we trying to solve? What are the constraints that exist? What are the dependencies?" When we validate a specific word such as 'and' or 'or' in the statement, it may bring more idea to clarify the core matters.

- Define problem

    - McKinsey's framework suggests the problem statement worksheet to aid in problem definition. Most of contents to fill in the worksheet require the thought processes and discussions generated as the team develops it. There are several ways to maximize this value under the perspective below.
    - Basic question
        - Make the basic question SMART[13]
    - Context
        - Sets out the situation and complication facing the client – e.g., industry trends, relative position in the industry.
    - Success criteria
        - Defines success for the project. Must be shared by client and team, and must include relevant qualitative and

---

[12] "How to master the seven-step problem-solving process", Sep.13.2019, Podcast, www.mckinsey.com
[13] Specific, Measurable, Action oriented, Relevant, and Time-bound

quantitative measures – e.g., impact and impact timing, visibility of improvement, client mindset shifts Make sure you understand how the client and the team define success and failure.

- Scope
    - Indicates what will and will not be included in the study – e.g., international markets, research and development activities, uncontrolled corporate costs
- Constraints within solution space
    - Defines the limits of the set of solutions that can be considered – e.g., must involve organic rather than inorganic growth and constraints.
- Stakeholders
    - Identifies who makes the decisions and who else could support (or derail) the study –e.g., CEO, division manager, business unit leader, key outside influencers.
- Key sources of insight
    - Identifies where knowledge, best-practice expertise, and engagement approaches exist (internal and client) – e.g., practice experts, engagement manager guides, practice databases

- Structure problem

- Suggest two most helpful techniques for rigorously structuring any problem are hypothesis trees and issue trees. Articulating the problem as hypotheses, rather than issues, is the preferred approach because it leads to a more focused analysis of the problem. Often, the team has insufficient knowledge to build a complete hypothesis tree at the start of an engagement. In these cases, it is best to begin by structuring the problem using an issue tree. An issue tree is best set out as a series of open questions in sentence form.

- **Prioritize issues**

  - Once the problem has been structured, the next step is to prioritize the issues or hypotheses on which the team will focus its work.

- **Plan analysis and work**

  - If the prioritization has been carried out effectively, the team will have clarified the key issues or hypotheses that must be subjected to analysis. The aim of these analyses is to prove the hypotheses true or false, or to develop useful perspectives on each key issue. Now the task is to design an effective and efficient workplan for conducting the analyses.

- Conduct analysis

    - The bulk of an engagement generally consists of gathering facts and conducting analyses to solve the problem.

- Synthesize findings

    - This is the most difficult element of the problem-solving process. After a period of being immersed in the details, it is crucial to step back and distinguish the important from the merely interesting. Distinctive problem solvers seek the essence of the story that will underpin a crisp recommendation for action.

- Develop recommendation

    - It is at this point that we address the client's questions: "What do I do, and how do I do it?" Elegantly synthesized analytical solutions are often not sufficient for client impact. Our clients tell us that we create great solutions and identify unique opportunities, but that we need to push our recommendations to a more actionable level. In addition, our own research suggests that clients often fail to capture the full benefits of our work, largely because of lack of organizational commitment and the skills required for execution.

Therefore, our work is incomplete until we have actionable recommendations, along with a plan and client commitment for implementation.

Milan model, International Labor Organization (1996)

ILO has developed Management Consulting as a guide which is a widely recognized reference for the art of management consulting. It suggests an extensive introduction with insights for a client as well as a consultant.

- Entry

    - A meeting between the client and the consultant takes place, and a consulting contract is established

through the preliminary diagnosis process.
- Initial meeting with the client
- Preliminary problem diagnosis
- Draft consulting execution plan
- Suggest consulting execution plan to clients
- Consulting contract

- Diagnosis

  - Problem and root cause are identified through in-depth research to clarify current issues compares to the goals to be achieved.
  - Analyze objective
  - Problem Analysis
  - Fact gathering and analysis
  - Feedback to clients

- Action Planning

  - Based on the problems and causes identified through the diagnosis process, alternatives are defined, and an action plan is established
  - Develop a solution
  - Evaluate the solution
  - Present solutions to clients
  - Develop an action plan

- Implementation

- Lead and promote change according to the established action plan
- Support execution
- Adjust solutions
- Training and communication

- Termination

  - Report on completion of consulting project and withdraw
  - Evaluation
  - Draft the final report
  - Follow-up work plan
  - Withdrawal

The book will elaborate the overall framework based on ILO (International Labor Organization) model, however other practices and trends will be also added for further details. As we have seen above, since the consulting performance methodology is based on the organizational change theory in the management field, the basic approaches and steps are like each other theory.

Recently, more efforts are being made to build the methodology as a framework for problem solving and to apply the most appropriate problem analysis and solution techniques to each step. It is just like there are some of the world's top-class POSCO[14] and Nippon Steel Corp[15], even if they produce the

---

[14] http://www.posco.com

same raw materials and similar processes, while there are steel mills that are unable to avoid losses. The methodology will be able to realize value when consultant has domain knowledge in the industry.

---

[15] http://www.nipponsteel.com

2. CONSULTING PROCESS

In the dictionary, a process means a series or set of activities that interact to produce a result; it may occur once only or be recurrent or periodic. Also, the process can repeat under predefined protocol with other processes, and process-driven consulting gives several benefits. For instance, process plays a common language between client and consultant. The process is a framework to make sure quality of consulting deliverables. Besides, the process provides utility to improve productivity and leverage knowledge assets.

In this chapter will briefly introduce key features of each step of consulting process according to the International Labor Organization model.

Initial contacts

A client is looking for an external consultant when they face challenges while they deal with problems. Also, they want to get independent advice when they need to get advice with expertise for stepping up. Usually, magazines, conferences, industry networking, and peer reviews will be sourced to get a consultant contacted.

But, in many cases, consultancy proposes workshops to discover challenges and define priorities with a client when the consultancy has enough information and experience. Eventually, the consultancy suggests consulting project based on the workshop, and it is common practice when a consulting firm does the business under tough competition. However, it is not the right way when the client is not aware of challenges, or they have another priority. Furthermore, it leads to a rigid relationship with a client and limits creative thinking over the whole project term. Also, a client may have a rather passive attitude and does not engage in the project actively. To avoid those happening, a consultant needs to keep asking a question about what, and why for now in order to make them having awareness of the objectives.

2.1 Entry

At this stage, it can be decided whether the consultancy accepts the statement of work (SOW) through an initial contact between the client and the consultant. Also, consulting services contract will be drafted upon the statement of work. The most important task of this stage is to discover and assess the objectives of consulting upon a mutual understanding with trust between client and consultant. Both must be on the same page for the future direction with a common vision, and interests.

First Meeting

The first meeting is set up by the consultant, and it is great momentum for the client to build a common trust with a positive impression of the consultant. The consultant's first meeting is critical for the client to have trust, confidence, and a positive impression of the consultant. At this time, it is effective for the consultant to present and explain similar and successful cases to build trust with the client. The consultant, who has judged the feasibility of the consulting project through the first meeting, decides whether to proceed with the preliminary diagnosis process.

A consultant leads the first meeting. It is necessary to understand the key factors centered on the characteristics of the industry in advance, including the client's organization and the business environment. It should be taken into account that the client does not want a readymade solution and wants a unique solution suitable for the company. The meeting materials to be used in the first meeting are prepared to consider below.

- Macroeconomy of the country where company does business
- Industry maturity and growth
- Domain-specific challenges
- Regulation, practices, and systems affecting to client's business
- Market competition
- Market position of the client in the industry
- Products and services what the client produce or sell
- Technology what the client utilizes for doing business

In many consulting firms, they are maintaining knowledge assets internally or subscriptions to data services externally. For the first meeting, the client expects to know whether the consultant is aware of common priorities in the industry domain and wants to discover thought leadership from the consultant. Consultant needs to manage expectation as the first meeting is not the place to meet everyone's expectations at one time and need to assess whether the client is aware of what issue either priority they have.

Selecting attendees and venue will be also an important consideration when the consultant plans the first meeting. If the client does expect to have a workshop that calls many stakeholders, a consultant needs to avoid a workshop as it is usually hard to build consensus through such a workshop unless the client has a clearly defined problem internally. Below tells several checkpoints while the consultant designs the first meeting.

Understand the client
- What are they doing in what environment?
- Which group shows the most interesting reaction to the?
- What function drives changes within the client organization internally?
- Who will be a key decision-maker?
- Has the client received the same or similar consulting services before?
- Has the client gotten consulting services from us in the past?
- With market or similar reference, what problem is expected?

Understand behavioral expectations of the client
- Does the client expect several rounds of initial meetings before beginning a consulting project or wants to initiate the project immediately? If then, will the client delegate full authority to the consultant to assess their capability?
- Is the client interested in radical innovations or trial and error?
- Does the client have a straightforward or more flexible against changes?

Readiness of consultant
- Does the consultant fully understand the priorities with objectives?
- Does the consultant understand the strategy and capabilities of the consulting firm where they are working? If then, is the consultant able to utilize knowledge assets which is maintained by the consulting firm?
- Is the consultant able to decide "Yes" or "No" upon strategic

---

value when he/she is asked to develop a solution?
- Does the consultant understand the methodology that they will apply?
- Considering expectations from the client, does the consulting firm mobilizes the best resources to lead the productive discussion?

If the consultant wants to answer "No" to a question from the client,
- As a consultant, can you clearly explain why?
- As a consultant, can you suggest alternatives?

DO at the first meeting

- Discovers feasibilities to develop valuable advantage through consulting project
- Assesses what level of awareness client has against problems that they have
- Listen to what client appeals
- Promote active discussion
- Manage expectations
- Keep confidentiality of consulting references
- Tell responsibility of each attendee
- Understand and clarify decision-maker, opinion leader, and influencer on the client's end

DON'T at the first meeting

- Avoid advice unless the consultant has confidence based on fact analysis
- Beware of stereotypes or prejudice

- Not to propose best-of-breed which does not align with the client's capability
- Not to persuade consulting project if the client is not ready
- Avoid providing too much information at once
- Not to share other client's deliverables without approval from them

Discover problems

Typically, key stakeholders of a client may concern and express what they are experiencing at their responsibility instead of having a holistic point of view. It is natural for them as it should be the most critical problem when the stakeholder runs operations at their end. However, a consultant needs to promote a multi-dimensional perspective instead of receiving, accepting, or challenging their perception. At the first meeting, a consultant does not have enough understanding to judge the problems that the client has or justify what solution will be applicable. While the first meeting, it will be a key takeaway to make clients having awareness of where they are at and what they need to think about changes. For instance, a consultant may need to ask several questions below to promote a more open and productive discussion at the meeting.

- What led you to such a conclusion?
- What are you ultimately interested in by an approach like this?

- You seem very impressed with 'ABC'. What do you think 'ABC' can solve your concerns?
- Do you think what concerns will be addressed by such an approach?
- I want to hear all the underlying issues you face today
- Let's take a step back and think from a different angle to address your concerns
- Please give me a few examples of your interests
- Please explain a different approach along with a macro view of this problem
- What are the benefits when you resolve these problems?
- When and where do you expect the concerns to be resolved?
- Do you think the existing process is working now?
- How do others perceive this issue?
- Can you give me background more about it?

Sometimes, attendees of the first meeting have a bit passive position or do not want to receive the changes. If it goes on, the consultant and key stakeholder will not be able to get the expected takeaway accomplished as those passive or negative impressions will bring invisible resistance within the client's organization internally before key stakeholder drives changes. At the same time, it will not be a good address to persuade either enforce the resistance directly other than making them self-motivated with awareness. If the client shows a passive attitude or does not want to change very much, the reason is as follows.

- When the attendee believes that the current practice is affordable as it is although it is not perfect
- The attendee does not think the benefit is not less than efforts when the change is deployed to him/her
- The attendee has another higher priority and is not able to allocate his resources to implement the changes
- The attendee does not have the confidence to work with the consultant

Preliminary Assessment

A preliminary assessment is like diagnosing a patient that a doctor visits for the first time. In the hospital, the doctor asks about symptoms, takes body temperature, listens to heartbeat, and takes samples for lab tests additionally when it is necessary. It is part of clarifying the cause of diseases in order to decide on treatment. It is not an actual treatment but a groundwork to gather initial facts for developing a hypothesis looking for a treatment.

Similarly, the consultant gets, listens, observes, and understands what the client faces with challenges through interviews, discussions, and existing documents while the first meeting. Also, it is the process to build consensus on why the client needs to have a consulting project. Simultaneously, it is the timing to develop a hypothesis about what methodology with the technique will be applied when the actual project is initiated. To manage expectations at the client end, it is important to highlight that the purpose of the preliminary assessment is not to present an exact solution to a problem.

A preliminary assessment has limited terms and resources under certain conditions. Typically, a preliminary assessment is completed within a week or less. However, it requires building and testing hypotheses upon data gathered at the first meeting and eventually verifying common objectives under common understanding. Besides, the preliminary assessment requires a bit of intensive work to structure consulting project plan based on business insight with domain knowledge.

In certain cases, it is able to skip the preliminary assessment and begin the consulting project directly if a client has clearly defined objectives and expected deliverables under agreed terms with a consulting firm. If a client does not have a clear understanding of the priority of problems, a consultant needs to suggest a preliminary assessment making more clarifications. Also, a consultant needs to highlight risk exposure if the consulting project begins with unclear objectives.

While the preliminary assessment, a consultant needs to utilize and maximize the existing data such as annual report, market report, key metrics, employee headcount with compensation, annual MBO report, regulation, industry compliance, a chronological event of business function (or regional business unit), and employee pulse survey (aka employee satisfaction survey).

The existing internal report gives perspective to an internal audience, and it has a more customized report based on in-depth data analytics. Comparing an internal report, market data provides a more comparable report according to industry metrics such as market share, mean time between failure, and most of the financial metrics. The external report gives data from more independent perspectives and benefits to analyze historical data at the same metric.

As qualitative data, the consultant usually utilizes interviews either surveys, but the consultant needs to consider several limitations according to questions architecture or population when utilizing existing reports of interviews or surveys.

If a consultant has a plan to circulate a survey, it is important to design questions under hypothesis and select the population in the right manner. Usually, as a preliminary assessment has a week term or less, a consultant does not want to lose their time for design questions, selecting respondents, reviewing data, and analyzing data.

Due to those limitations, a consultant may consider group discussions such like a focus group interview, a workshop, public hearing, or town hall meetings. Group discussion brings more open communication with reality, but it does have risks caused by different levels of perception/bias of opinion leaders. A consultant does not need to drive discussions toward results but needs to promote a discussion in a productive manner.

One of the critical factors which will affect the quality of the preliminary assessment will be staffing for the assessment. If a senior executive is a key attendee of the assessment, consulting firm needs to select a consultant who has industry insights and market intimacy. If functional leadership is a key attendee of the assessment, consulting firm needs to assign a consultant who is able to present and persuade market practice based on key metrics.

In any case, a consultant should have the capability to listen to what the attendee explains, understand what problem the client faces, moderate active discussion, and summarize what has been discussed. Communication skill is one of the most important factors when consulting firm selects a consultant for the assessment. Although the consultant knows with experience, it will not be effective if the consultant cannot communicate appropriately with key stakeholders while the assessment.

Identify business requirements

In the case of government agencies or social welfare institutions that require public interest, the following checklist may not be completely met. Excludes non-profit organizations, the following question is applicable when a consultant understands and identifies business requirements.

- Clarify business challenges

    - What has brought this challenge? Please explain the background.
    - What is the expected benefit and objectives of this project?
    - What business challenges are expected to be

resolved after the project?
- What resolution have the clients tried so far?
- Can you consider the project from a different perspective?

• Clarify expectations with responsibility when a client engages in the project

- What client expects output of the consulting project?
- Please recommend candidates for project resources
- Who knows with experience within the organization?
- Does your organization have a committee or council to collaborate across functions?
- What if you face resistance while driving changes, how can you make it resolve the issue or conflicts?
- Do you have any principle or bottom line to promote changes?
- What is your definition of success after the project?
- What will your definition of failure be after the project?
- Can you provide several expected risks when you deploy changes?

In order to refine business requirements or clarify the objectives of a consulting project, the consultant needs to promote productive discussion under multi-dimensional perspectives. For instance, the shareholder is easily asking to improve market share and wants to define what factor has brought the current market share. Although market share is a proven metric in the industry, there are a lot of concerns with different positions such like population, term, and definition of the market.

Plus, there will be many different factors when each business stakeholder interprets the facts. Sales directors may look for a reason from the supply chain why they were not able to gain more market share. At the same time, the production team may complain demand volatility has added more burden to operation. Similarly, the strategy team may look for the reason from brand awareness or IT applications.

Consultant needs to appreciate all suggestions from the attendee while a preliminary assessment and remind them to have wide bandwidth of understanding of the existing process.

Here are some guidelines on how to define the problem in the preliminary assessment.

- When the problem is general or expressed in unclear

  - Understand the structure of a problem
  - Visualize unclear matters in order to get it defined or classified
  - Evaluate the priority or interdependency among the visualized matters
  - Example)
    - Client: "We have an issue associated with messaging software capabilities"
    - Consultant: "Can you tell me just a few key things about the software

problems you experienced when you utilize it for daily operation?", "When you state the problem, will it be different than your expectations or defined throughput of your MBO[16]?"

- When the problem describes too many broad challenges

  - Ask the client to show a specific example
  - Ask questions about the business issues underlying problems
  - Advise client to elaborate problems upon several different dimension
  - Example)
    - Client: "The existing call center application does not work to address customer concerns"
    - Consultant: "Can you explain what trouble customer experiences brought by call center application?", "Do you think what specific features of call center application have to be improved? Process? Data integrity? Reliability?"

- When the client states the problem in a narrow bandwidth

---

[16] MBO, Management by Objectives

- Ask the client to make sure whether the problem has happened sporadically
- Encourage to use a bigger framework while the client shapes problems
- Highlights the problems with a new angle
- Example)
  - Client: "ERP[17] process does not give benefits to me. It requires huge efforts in an unproductive manner."
  - Consultant: "What benefits are you expecting from ERP process?", "Do you believe whether ERP process can cover key functionalities of most of all applications?"

- If the problem needs to be reevaluated

  - Compare pros and cons, and highlight improvement if the change is deployed
  - Build consensus for desired state and current challenges
  - Example)
    - Client: "We need to mobilize and run task forces resolving issues intensively"
    - Consultant: "I understand you believe concentrated efforts will improve key metrics significantly. However, it will

---

[17] Enterprise Resource Planning

be important to mobilize resources and make sure initiatives upon the problems". "To accomplish improvement by running the task forces, I do recommend you make sure whether the resources are aware of the problem on the same page with key stakeholders"

Set the target to achieve thru consulting project

A client may be eager to resolve the challenges, improve the business processes, and achieve key performance indicators by implementing initiatives after consulting. Although many stakeholders want to achieve the target, there will be different levels of achievement upon each one's perception. Someone does want to improve by phase and highlights moderate resistance. At the same time, another stakeholder may want to improve significantly by running initiatives in radical approaches. Also, they may believe they can take a risk brought by the resistance of stakeholders as timing to change will be more important than anything.

Usually, a client wants to consider industry benchmarks, competitor's references, or internal justification when they set the target whether it is indicators, metrics, or YoY comparison.

For instance, company A produces passenger vehicles

in county X. They want to reduce new product development lead time. Currently, they have 50 months spent starting from idealization, concept design, and pilot test to official launch after completing all quality inspections. They want to reduce the lead time to less than 36 months. Consultant needs to make sure whether the definition of new product development lead time is typically agreed upon and applied in the industry. If not, a client will be hard to compare their target as well as achievements with industry benchmarks.

In a different case, company B keeps reducing inventory to improve financial conditions as their current turnover is at 0.65 per year. For this case, a consultant needs to identify the bandwidth of inventories for turnover calculation in the warehouse.

Each service part has a different lifecycle, and the market demand is related to the conditions of the vehicles that the user has. The warehouse manager wants to compare their metrics with benchmarks on the same page. However, the manager may be wondering to clarify what materials will be when they calculate a turnover ratio. Will it be a whole parts group or parts selected that has a high turnover rate in the last year? Will it be compared with benchmarks of the same or similar industry?

Another client may expedite their changes with aspirations instead of reality. These clients consider and look for opportunities to realize the changes by acquiring resources, talents, capabilities, customers, and markets. It may be an effective decision when the client gets into an emerging market or diversified industry that requires time-to-market rather than any other unique capabilities. Someone calls it an aspiration-driven approach or inorganic approach.

If a client wants to set the target according to their internal judgment, a consultant may need to highlight that prerequisite may affect the achievement later. Sometimes, the client may want to set a target upon their current capabilities under manageable risk. Someone calls it a resource-based approach or on organic approach.

Develop consulting project plan

According to the preliminary assessment, a consultant develops a project plan for a decision-maker who will buy it and provide sponsorship under commitment. The decision-maker will drive changes, play a role as a champion to define the desired state, and finally accept the changes for the business operation when the project is on.

The plan briefly states business challenges against the desired state, target value for the key indicators, and tasks to complete over the project. The details are as below.

- Problems or challenges identified
- Objectives of the consulting project
- Expected benefits achieved by the project
- Project scope
- Project timeline includes key events
- Required resources
- Budget
- Expected risk
- Expected sponsorship

When the decision-maker agrees and accepts the project plan, a consultant will be asked to provide a proposal. However, if the decision-maker wants to select a consultancy over a bidding process, the project plan will be one of reference when the client drafts RFP Request for Proposal. The client refines and revises the project plan and adds below to the drafted RFP.

- Background and expectations of the project
- Business challenges and requirements in overall
- Scope, required tasks with deliverables
- Acceptance criteria of deliverables
- Vendor selection criteria and process
- Code of compliance and non-disclosure agreement

Reviews the proposal

The proposal is a critical document directly related to getting a project win for a consulting company. The proposal requires clearly described contents, refined tasks such as DO and DON'T, and more quantitative items to help the client's decision-making. Besides, a consultant needs to consider or include the below when they develop a proposal for RFP.

- Business philosophy and history of client
- Market intelligence
- Industry practice
- Clients' internal organizations, management style, and cultural characteristics
- Atmosphere, awareness of challenges within the client organization
- Brief information on consulting methodologies
- Data sources to be utilized through consulting project
- Recommended decision criteria for decision-maker of client
- Required support or responsibilities of the client
- Risk or issue management
- Communication strategy
- Resource plan
- Consultant profile includes experiences
- Cost projection and pricing strategy of the project
- Key advantages compared with other consultancies

Before sending the proposal to the client, there would be an additional internal procedure to be completed within the consultancy. It will be different by each consultancy upon the internal process. Proposed tasks and deliverables upon their preliminary assessment will be a part of the proposal. At the same time, the other important part should be as below.

As a profit organization, consulting firm also needs to get enough level of profit for making sure financial healthy. It does mean that consulting proposal needs to bill the professional charges upon market price.

- Cost estimates; Labor cost, travel expenses, other expenses of the events such as workshops, interviews, surveys, research, pilot modeling, etc.

- Quotation; Price simulation under several scenarios in order to meet financial healthy. It includes payment conditions upon acceptance criteria.
- Contingency; Add a certain amount of project cost upon risk profile. The quality assurance manager assesses the risk rate of the project and allocates additional costs just in case of project delay, or unknown risks.

- Consultant compensation; Add the amount of project cost for consultant retention. It spends as a utilization bonus, winning bonus, or benefit sharing.

A consulting service contract will be able to execute when the client approves the statement of work proposed by the consultancy. All the proposed terms and conditions will be part of a contract, and it requires a procedure of internal compliances before the consulting firm finally confirms and sends the proposal to the client.

- Regulation or compliance: In the industry, several regulatory restrictions may bring tough challenges that are not able to manage by the client. For instance, manufacturing companies consider and adopt ISO regulations. Financial institutions report and maintain documents according to SEC regulations. An automaker has to keep service parts maintained for 10 years.

- Early termination: If the consultancy either client quits the project without mutual agreement, the termination penalty may be billed according to the agreed terms and conditions in the contract.

- Indemnification: Unexpected, unknown risk may bring a lawsuit to both a consulting firm and a client. Sometimes, it may easily exceed the contract amount depending on the agreed terms and conditions. To prevent these expected risks, the consulting firm applies predefined terms and conditions for indemnification, and the proposal committee reviews the proposal before consulting firm officially submits it to the client.

- Intellectual property: Consultant may utilize market data, competitor references, and client's internal assets. However, it has an unknown risk unless the consultant correctly cites and uses the data. Both consulting firm and client may need to sign the nondisclosure agreement not to utilize intellectual assets in inappropriate manner.

- Warranty: The client may be concerned about the effectiveness of a report if they realize the plan is not working to implement. However, it is not simply clarified whether the defect is clearly under the consultant's responsibility if a client has accepted the report in each step. For instance, company X has developed a performance-driven marketing program that utilizes personal advertising identity on mobile devices. While client implements apps, they realize that they cannot collect location data from the mobile device unless the user allows them to share personal data, and it returns poor accomplishment of change as a result. For this case, it will be the consultant's responsibility if a consultant has not researched influences brought by data privacy regulation. To prevent this challenge, consulting firm designs and sets warranty processes over the project term when they deliver reports.

When a proposal is ready, a proposal council reviews the items below before they finally confirm it with quote details.

- Risk assessment: Terms, conditions, requirements, technical maturity, experience, regulation, and competition may be critical factors to validate the risk exposure, and it will affect contingency or bring the decision not to submit a bid.

- Change control process: Upon the agreed protocol, the statement of work is officially revised, and it will make the scope, responsibilities, and incremental cost clear.

- Issue escalation: Depending on the severity of the issue, it should be reported to right contact and escalated to ownership for getting a decision respectively.

Technically, consulting firm mobilizes a task force to prepare a proposal. Typically, the task force will be engaged as project team members when the firm wins the deal. The task force is composed of several different responsibilities such as below.

- Proposal lead who usually forms proposal skeleton and manages resources while proposal term

- Subject matter expert who drafts a plan for tasks, deliverables, and required events over the projects

- Quality assurance manager who needs to review and make sure that the proposal is appropriate upon given conditions such like client's requirements, budget, and timeline

- Documentation and librarian

A proposal is not a thesis or an article. It is a selling document that describes what, why, and how with confidence to the client. Finally, a proposal lead reviews the proposal if it addresses the client's requirements and provides confidence. The proposal is approved by a client when it delivers a well-organized project strategy with priorities. A client may not be an expert to understand quickly what consulting services they will get. The proposal should address a key message in a clear tone and manner. Examples of considerations are as follows.

- Should be written in common terminologies and easy to understand
- Visualize the key implications when delivering statistics
- Justification with rationale
- Client's responsibility
- Answer for questions expected

For your reference, the further criterion to review a proposal are listed below. The proposal review board or quality assurance verifies the proposal with the criteria below before consulting firm finally submits it to the client.

- Objectives of consulting
  - Make sure the approach is effective to resolve problems that the client has
  - Assure the project aligns with the client's business mission, objectives, and aspiration

---

THE BASICS OF CONSULTING PROCESS

- Scope of the project proposed
    - Any missing item
    - Verify the balance and dependencies among tasks proposed

- Expected improvements thru the project
    - Effectiveness of process, product, and services as part of project deliverables
    - Confirm whether the definition of success is close to the client's expectation
    - Will it be able to suggest a significant improvement of key performance indicator?
    - Complete risk assessment before confirming task with resource allocation

- Quality of services
    - Make sure the project plan maintains quality assurance in each key event
    - What will be the acceptance criteria?
    - Escalation process

- Resource to utilize through the project
    - Utilizes the most valuable knowledge asset
    - Mobilize internal/external advisory if necessary
    - Qualification of project member

- Project timeline
    - Verification of key paths with tasks
    - Validate project term whether it is enough to complete all proposed tasks

- Given constraints
    - Client's financial conditions

- - Resources availability of client
  - Regulation
  - Other constraints and resources

- • Key stakeholders of clients
  - Have key stakeholders identified
  - Reflect key stakeholders' interests or concerns
  - Decision maker

- • Communication
  - Communication channel and protocol by stakeholder
  - Report-out session and attendee

- • Change management
  - How to drive changes
  - Problem and conflict management

Below tells several lessons learned while the author has experienced the project.

- • Guiding principles

  - A proposal is the toolkit for communication
  - Avoid describing super details
  - Develop a proposal easy to read
  - Be aware of thought-flow, and logical dependency to elaborate the storyline
  - Do not highlight too many specific examples either reference
  - Keep thinking to align with the interests of a client

- Proposal is not for selling knowledge asset, but for realizing the objective by utilizing the knowledge assets

- Soft skill to deliver a message

  - Inductive approach is more effective than the deductive proposal. But the deductive approach is effective when a consultant drafts a hypothesis in the project
  - Need to show consultant understands needs and wants of a client, but wants to focus on the priorities
  - Make a client sitting on the same page as you. Or, make them have the awareness that a consultant is sitting on the same page with them
  - Make sure whether the proposal has a missing piece comparing items of RFP
  - Validate the proposal addresses the requirements of RFP
  - Logically emphasizes why what for now.
  - Assess and simulate whether the task/events will be able to complete within the term. Consulting project is not a research project.
  - Make clients have confidence in their awareness of reality and motivation to change

Submit the proposal

Many clients generally accept a proposal in electronic format instead of hard copies. Usually, the government organization asks that the consultancy submits a proposal with evidence documents at the procurement portal. Sometimes, a consulting firm prefers to submit a hard copy as well as an electronic format of the proposal because they believe that it will bring more interest from the client. Each consulting firm has a different pricing scheme; however, the client usually asks for cost details by item. The price offer has to indicate an expiration date, currency with tax details.

Competing process

Typically, a client has an internal process to evaluate and select the right partner upon the proposal. Although the evaluation process is a little different by case, it usually takes a series of validation tasks such as proposal review, presentation, interview, and reference review. The price offer is also important in the decision criteria once the proposal meets the requirements. Upon the number of bidders, a client runs several rounds of evaluation processes to select the partner efficiently. If a client has received the proposal from five candidates, they pick up 2 out of 5 candidates in the first round and run the 2nd round for two candidates in detail.

Although the consultant expects that client will select the best proposal if the content meets all requirements, it is required to understand the different interests of each stakeholder. For instance, management leadership tries to verify business impact if they implement it. Functional leadership may want to validate whether the consultant will be easy to collaborate with their employee in the project. Also, they expect their people to get capabilities improved by learning knowledge and experience from the consultant. Finally, the board of directors may focus on the returns on investment if it brings an upfront cost. It does mean that each party has questions with different backgrounds, so consulting firm needs to address the expectation in the proposal or deliver the solutions in the presentation session.

To get confidence from the proposal, a client wants to validate it based on the reference that has done by the bidder. Consultant needs to be aware that it is the consultancy's intellectual property and be able to share the reference under the previous client's approval. If the client does not want to share it, a consultant cannot prepare an interview or site visit for the client.

Although it may be varied by project, a consulting firm needs to notify the expiration of a proposal because resource utilization is a critical measure in operating a consulting organization.

Contract

When an entry phase does meet the client's expectation, the final last step will be a contract project under agreed terms and conditions. Each signing party will be able to suggest their standard terms and conditions as a template, and the legal counsel of each end negotiates the languages for making a mutual agreement.

LOA(Letter of Agreement) is usually regarded as a contract although it is not an official contract. It states the scope of work with the responsibilities of each end. The LOA or official contract called SOW is valid under the master service agreement which describes standard terms and conditions as a bottom line.

As per the billing scheme, both ends will be able to agree with the protocol upon the project. If it has uncertainty about the scope or deliverables, time and material contract will be an applicable scheme. If the deliverables are clearly defined, and the client has knowledge about risks, a lump sum contract may be preferred. If the project has too many risks or does not have enough references, a client may be able to propose sharing the benefit instead of applying a traditional contract scheme.

In the case of MNC(Multi-National Company), the geographical scope will be also important when consulting firm confirms the terms and conditions. If the contract states that a consultant needs to gather the voice of customer from each geographical territory, will it be a global project or a local project? If it is a global project across the region, a consulting firm needs to allocate the resources by region. In another case, if a client emphasizes improvement of the global supply chain although the project will be done in the States, are you able to clarify what expectations with risks will come together for the scope?

Below tells the typical contents of a contract.

- Contract entity

  - Company governance includes the relationship b/w parent company and child companies are important. It may be related to who will be able to access and utilize the deliverable after the project

- Scope of work

  - Task, event, session, and deliverables will be a major part of the scope
  - Acceptance criteria and deliverables of task
  - Resources plan includes external advisory
  - Work schedule or timeline.
  - A key event of the timeline should be tied to the sign-off process which will bring an invoicing process

- Cost strategy

  - Resource cost
  - Expenses for travel, event, research, and others
  - Insurance
  - Tax

- Legal notice

- Intellectual property
- Responsibility
- Issue escalation process
- Indemnification

In some cases, multiple parties can get the award when a client wants to select multiple partners instead of a single firm. For this case, a client typically selects one as a dedicated primary vendor and asks them to make a subcontract with the other candidates which has been selected by a client. If the client strongly asks to make the subcontract on behalf of them, a consulting firm needs to assess the risk and mitigation. However, it will be a better way if a client makes a separate contract with the other consultancy or makes a three-parties contract.

There are several items below that consultants should pay attention to and check during the contracting process.

- Has the contract appropriately stated the background, expectations, and objectives?
- Any misalignment or possible misleading of the scope described in the contract?
- What are the client's roles and responsibilities over the project in general?
- Communication and approval process while the project
- Business classified information
- How to mediate concerns or conflicts?
- Who owns this project within the client organization?
- Does the client assign the best resources to the project?

- Who is responsible for executing the sign-off of the contract?
- Who owns the deliverables? Who can use the deliverables?
- Who is responsible for accepting the deliverables? What will be the acceptance criteria?
- What are the start and end date of the project?
- Have key events been identified and agreed upon with the client?
- Commitment from management leadership

2.2 Diagnosis

The diagnosis process is running to assess the current state upon the objectives of a consulting project. To evaluate the status correctly, a consultant needs to set the aspiration against the current state, and it will provide ideas when identifying problems. The definition of a problem from the client's perspective is important because it may be varied by expectation, and the problems according to its definition with criteria will be a baseline before the consultant goes toward an in-depth diagnosis process. Typically, the consultant can apply several different methodologies for the diagnosis process to get root causes identified.

For instance, many life insurance companies maintain the cancellation rates of a new policy at 13 months old as a key metric. If the rate goes up significantly than expected, each stakeholder has a different interpretation of their business function. The product team analyzes the root cause with the point of risk rate, an interest rate, or even unemployment rate from the external environment. At the same time, the customer service center they are willing to analyze the accomplishment in the view of customer experience, and mobile app service ownership tries to understand whether their mobile app was able to bring attention from the policyholder.

Typically, the project team should analyze anything related to the problems. A consultant discovers a root cause of the problem including their interrelationships among the causes because there is no single solid root cause for the problem. Consultant needs to identify problems under the agreed definition and analyze the root cause upon the objectives of a consulting project. However, it is important to make all stakeholders aware that it is not a productive approach if the project team gathers and analyzes every detail, every inch, and every penny from all perspectives.

The diagnosis process gives implications to all stakeholders because it provides the moment bringing a common interest such as where they are, what they have, and what they need to get by when. Plus, those facts with root causes should be shared with stakeholders as part of change management because the stakeholder usually wants to know whether the consultant has analyzed facts with necessary and sufficient conditions. If a stakeholder judges the perspectives or approaches are not aligned with their business practices, they will not approve the changes during the implementation. That is the reason why the consultant needs to consider strategic thought leadership.

Strategic thought leadership

Strategic thought leadership leverages systematics thinking as well as creative thinking.

Systematic thinking is a thought process of analyzing facts and discovering root causes based on logical thinking. It makes a consultant generate analytics if a consultant takes a predefined procedure although they do not have enough knowledge or experience. It brings benefits to the project team by utilizing resources at maximum capacity, and it will be able to apply for quantitative analysis such as market survey, quality defects analysis, tear-down analysis, etc. Also, it makes the team delivers a quality report consistently.

Creative thinking is another approach to bringing an initiative out based on implicit knowledge, inspiration, out-of-box thinking, convergence across domains, etc. However, it returns a different implication depending on the consultant's capabilities. Furthermore, there is no formalized or standardized procedure to generate initiatives, and not able to produce a report consistently with this approach.

For instance, if a startup business has invented the most advanced technology, the market prospect is not big enough to get it returning when they consider investing what they have already spent in the last several years. Maybe the stakeholder will be concerned about the lower attractiveness of market growth, or industry experts may be looking for an opportunity within the existing industry if they do not want to take a risk based on their experiences.

As per multimedia streaming services, who will be a competitor and what will be a replacement? Will it be an entertainment player such as AMC theater? Or, will it be a traditional broadcasting system? It may be hard to define and analyze the industry landscape if it is an emerging business model.

Creative thinking is usually applied for this business case and brings out initiatives by redefining the existing industry.

Systematic thinking

A system tells a group or set of interrelated components that work together under a process with a holistic point of view. To get more details of systematic thinking, we need to understand the key features of the systems listed below.

- System runs from input, runs the process, and returns an output
- System needs to be understood as a whole set instead of a specific part of a set
- System may have subsystems
- Each subsystem has an organic interrelationship with other subsystems

- Subsystem generates synergy brought by interacting with other subsystems

With these features, systematic thinking makes a consultant analyze facts based on the logical thinking approach with holistic perspectives. It provides the most effective framework for decision-making when the decision maker has to deal with competing priorities under complicated interdependencies.

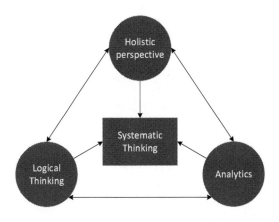

Systematic thinking is applicable for clarifying root causes as well as developing opportunities, and a consultant can verify all necessities and sufficient considerations not to skip critical components while the diagnosis phase.

Traditionally, there was active research in quality management, operation management, and value management to generate a report based on systematic thinking. As a result, a various toolkit has been developed and applied, and below tells several examples of toolkits.

- Issue tree

    - Developed by McKinsey & Company
    - Can apply for diagnosis as well as resolution
    - Diagnostic trees break down a "Why" key question, identifying all the possible root causes for the problem. Solution trees break down a "How" key question, identifying all the possible alternatives to fix the problem.

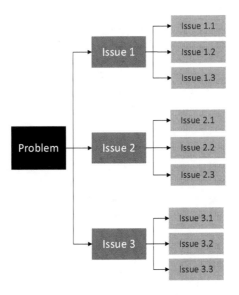

- Bayesian theorem

    - P(A|B) is a conditional probability: the probability of event A occurring given that B is true. It is also called the posterior probability of A given B.
    - P(B|A) is also a conditional probability: the probability of event B occurring given that A is true.
    - A and B must be different events.

$$P(A \mid B) = \frac{P(B \mid A)P(A)}{P(B)}$$

- Matrix analysis
  - Identify both dimensions exclusively and describe key features in each cell
    - i.e.) Market dynamics of construction equipment by customer segment

	Business	Government
Agriculture	Draught brought poor demand	State government considers a financing plan to encourage equipment replacement
Commercial buildings	Strong demand brought by shared office business	N/A
Infrastructure	N/A	Governor intends to renovate road and bridge
Landscaping	New town in construction	Resident files a petition for improving flooding protection
Mining	Strong demand for mineral	Government does not want to permit a license for new mining company due to pollution
Forestry	N/A	NGO concerns against new development
Ground maintenance	N/A	Local government plans to renovate

- Kawakita Jiro Method

91

- Capture whatever idea through brainstorming
- Group ideas by affinity or defined interests
- Label and consolidate ideas

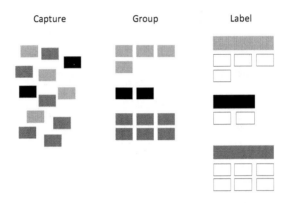

- Fishbone diagram (called Ishikawa diagram)
  - Invented by Kaoru Ishikawa
  - Break down root causes that bring problem out
  - In Manufacturing, 5 Ms stands for[18] Manpower, Machine, Measurement, Material, Method
  - Product marketing, 8 Ps are Product, Price, Place, Promotion, People, Process, Proof, Performance
  - For assessing business capability, 7 Ss should be[19] Strategy, Structure, System, Staff, Skill, Style, Shared Value

---

[18] Toyota Production System
[19] 7S Framework, McKinsey & Company

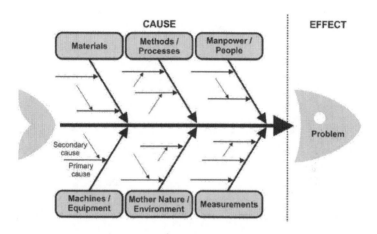

A consultant utilizes a toolkit as it gives several benefits as follows.

- Make a consistent analysis according to the structured process
- A toolkit is an effective protocol when communicating the findings to stakeholders
- Can be compared with other analysis

When a consultant educates and guides stakeholders to draft a report by leveraging a toolkit, it is important to make sure that the analysis has been done with MECE[20] perspectives.

---

[20] Mutually Exclusive Collectively Exhaustive

Creative thinking

Problem

A problem says a gap in the status compared with the desired state and is typically brought by multiple causes instead of one solid reason. Also. the cause has affected other causes. Each stakeholder has a different level of acceptance or awareness of the problem. Someone may be sensitive to a problem; however, the other stakeholders may not be sensitive to the same problem.

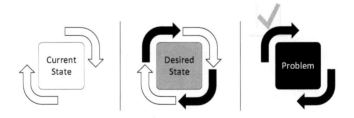

So, it is important to consider the types of the problem before getting into more details about them. For scope, impact, and feature of the problem, can be categorized below according to Peter Drucker[21].

---

[21] The Essential Drucker: The Best of Sixty Years of Peter Drucker's

- Truly a generic problem. It is more likely a common problem for most of the stakeholders as a structural problem.

- Generic problem, but unique for the individual. The problem is usually associated with process or structure, but it has a different magnitude of impact on stakeholders.

- Exceptionally unique problem. It requires in-depth investigation to clarify root causes, however, a consultant needs to consider the impact with priorities of a problem if it keeps going forward.

- Early manifestation of new generic problem. It is rarely observed throughout the diagnosis phase unless a consultant has domain knowledge at an excellent level.

In another category, there is a tendency to identify a problem according to the feasibility of implementation as below.

- Known problem, and it has a solution that requires just action. For this case, a consultant needs to drive change management with key metrics to encourage implementation.

- Known problem, however, requires subject matter expertise. For this case, a consultant needs to develop an action plan practically and train stakeholders to make it work by themselves. If it takes a long time or requires the expertise temporarily, a consultant can arrange an implementation partner.

- Known problem, but it requires a creative approach to break through fundamental challenges. Recently, a consultant looked for opportunities by leveraging technology to overcome.

- Unknown problem, even consultant or stakeholder does not recognize whether it is a problem. It requires in-depth research as discovery.

For business impact, problems are also categorized below[22].

- Risk: Possible downsides or negative outcomes stakeholders may face. Risks can be mitigated by identifying possible risks when the action is taken by

---

[22] Business Innovation Design,
https://businessinnovation.design/blog/2015/3/23/3-types-of-problems

stakeholders and developing solutions that prevent them from happening.

- Example: The production plan will not be working as expected when a material is not available as planned.

- Obstacle: Blockages that are slowing down and preventing progress or achieving goals.

  - Example: One of the vendors has not delivered parts, and the production team was not able to assemble a truck. The parts are commonly required in most assembly lines.

- Negative impact: Unwanted circumstances, problems, and consequences. It requires solutions that minimize negative impacts or turn around the situation from negative to positive.

  - Example: Business was not able to deliver a truck before the committed date and will have to pay a penalty charge.

Consultant needs to pay more attention to getting problem defined with critical perspectives. Also, it is highly recommended to make stakeholders aware of problems that the consultant defines at the diagnosis phase. Sometimes, stakeholder does like to identify problems within their knowledge with experiences, and they used to bring out many problems in their daily operations instead of a holistic perspective. The categories proposed above are useful for a consultant not to miss critical points and make balance keeping over the whole business process. In most cases, stakeholder experiences that it is not easy to classify symptom, problems, and causes as they've thought.

Key considerations encouraging active engagement while defining problems

When a consultant identifies a problem, there is a possibility of mistranslation influenced by stereotypes, groupthink, or subjective analysis. Typically, a consultant knows the difference between symptoms and problems. Although a consultant can discover the root causes from facts gathered, they should validate their findings upon the domain expertise. Below tell several cases that may be experienced when a consultant assesses the problem.

- Intuitive or subjective judgment depends on personal experiences only. No verified relationships between symptoms/facts.

    - For instance, the price is one of the factors when a consultant analyzes market behavior. Product support, residual value, and maintenance cost will also affect the decision. In other words, a premium price would not be the only reason for the lost deal, and the consultant needs to evaluate the price compared with the value that buyer was eager to get.

- Statistical analysis was not sufficient as the population has sampling error, standard error.

  - For getting implications from statistical analysis, the consultant needs to review and verify whether the population contains all required data points in alignment with objectives of the analysis.

- Perceptional bias or stereotype is brought by the loud.

  - They may have a clear opinion, but it will not be an answer to all questions. They may highlight symptoms or observations according to the frequency of events instead of the magnitude of business impact. The company may be sensitive to defect rates rather than quality costs. It will be important for resource management, but a standardized process with documentation will be more important.

Understand the interviewee's behavior

While the diagnosis phase, a consultant needs to maneuver atmospheres with tones and manner for more active participation of the interviewee. It is generally known that an interviewee's style brings influences overall achievements. Merrill & Roger[23] have suggested two dimensions to classify the social style of interviewees.

- Assertiveness: A person's behaviors are observed by others as forceful or directive.

- Responsiveness: A person's behaviors are recognized by others as emotionally controlled. More responsive people react noticeably to their own emotions or the emotions of others. Less responsive people are more guarded in their emotional expressions.

Those two dimensions make four clusters representing characteristics of personality. Below highlights the key feature and required skills of the cluster[24] to bring active engagement.

---

[23] Merrill & Roger, "Personal Styles and Effective Performance - 1981"
[24] Cited from Timur Tiryaki Basari Akademisi
http://www.timurtiryaki.com

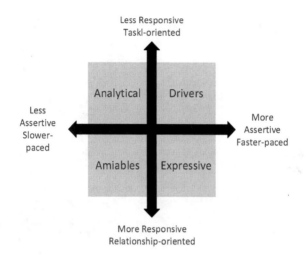

Driver

Key features	Soft skills to apply
Objective-focused Know what they want, how to get there Communicates quickly, gets to the point Sometimes tactless and brusque "Ends justify the means" type of person	Delivers objectives of interview Address implication of interview Get to core and direct question They don't want chit chat. Be short and to the point.

Expressive

Key features	Soft skills to apply
Natural salesmen or storyteller. Warm and enthusiastic Good motivators, communicators Can be competitive Tend to exaggerate and leave out facts Talk about things than do them	Show interest in interviewee Be careful not to miss key agenda

Amiable

Key features	Soft skills to apply
Kind-hearted people who avoid conflict Can blend into any situation well Can appear wishy-washy Has difficulty with firm decisions Can be quiet and soft-spoken	Ice breaking before interview. They won't raise a fuss but needs assurance if a problem arises Begins with a soft question

Analytical

Key features	Soft skills to apply
Highly detail-oriented people Difficult to decide without all the facts Make great accounts and engineers Tend to be highly critical people Can tend to be pessimistic in nature Very perceptive	Avoid ambiguous question. If a problem arises, they will keep asking questions till they are satisfied. Not preoccupied with a little thing

Data gathering strategy

Data gathering is the groundwork for analyzing current challenges and identifying the root causes. Besides, it is an important task to collect quality data aligning with objectives for getting an implication with a rationale. So, data gathering would be one of the critical success factors of quality analysis and can apply for multi-dimensional verification of hypothesis set by a consultant in a preliminary assessment phase. Below lists several procedures of data gathering.

- Determine what data you want to gather

  - The first thing to do is select what details a consultant wants to collect, and a consultant needs to draft a data point under the hypothesis under the initial assessment. At the same time, a consultant may need to consider whether a team can get the data with manageable efforts within a limited time. The objectives of consulting will determine the answers to these questions.
  - As an example, company A has recently started a consulting project to develop a strategy for nurturing prospects, and a consultant expects to get implications from data analysis. They set the objective of data analysis to identify the behavior of prospects by channel. Finally, a consultant decided to analyze entire sales leads sent by the client's public websites since last year.

- Set a timeline for data gathering

  - A consultant needs to define a timeline for gathering data. For example, a consultant may want to set up a method for tracking that data over the long term such as transaction data and website visitor data. It will be able to gather data effectively when a consultant specifies the conditions of sampling the data.

- If a consultant tracks data for a specific campaign, a consultant will track it over a defined period. If it can get raw data for the entire service year, it will be helpful to analyze interdependencies among quality defects. However, it will require significant effort to gather, verify, and organize mass data exponentially.

- Determine data gathering method

    - At this step, a consultant chooses the data-gathering strategy. In the case of internal data, a consultant needs to get support from a client for data extraction. If a consultant decides to circulate a survey as a gathering method, it will be important to design a questionnaire and define the population. In other cases, a consultant may be able to buy market data, if they can get sophisticated data quickly at a reasonable cost.
    - A consultant sometimes decides to collect data by observing operations in the line of business if they cannot find data properly. For this case, a consultant needs to pay more attention to keeping consistency when s/he judges raw data collected. For instance, a consultant observes workflow to find an unproductive task in the assembly line, however, it may be subjective to judge

unproductive tasks by comparing standard operation processes as each tasker has a different level of knowledge or experience.

- If a consultant considers analyzing mass data with statistical analysis, it is important to select an effective sampling strategy among random sampling, systematic sampling, stratified sampling, or cluster sampling. In case of non-probability sampling, maybe a consultant gets advice from an advisory on what sampling method will be appropriate among different gathering methods such as random sampling, purposive sampling, quota sampling, etc.

- Gather and analyze the data

   - Once all data is ready, it's time to analyze and organize the findings. Data analysis is a crucial process because it turns raw data into valuable insights that a consultant can use to get implications with root causes. It makes eventually brings future direction out according to key findings. All the analytics should be aligned with the objectives of a consulting project.

   - In case of statistical analysis, a consultant tests the hypothesis which has been set while preliminary assessment and needs to verify whether the statics has a statistical error. For instance, type 1 or type 2 error are often found while the consultant interprets statistics.

      ▪ Example: A patient gets tested for

COVID-19. Two errors that could potentially occur:

- Type 1 error (False positive); the test result says the patient has coronavirus, but the patient does not.
- Type 2 error (False negative); the test result says the patient does not have coronavirus, but the patient does.

Data analysis

While analyzing data, a consultant looks for an effective way to validate the hypothesis which has been set on preliminary assessment. Although both deductive and inductive approaches can apply to the hypothesis, a consultant needs to review and validate the quality of data before initiating actual analysis in advance. Several items below should be assessed.

- Completeness

  - All mandatory fields must be collected with minimum bandwidth of missing data. For instance, historical sales order has to have customer, item detail, pricing conditions, and document date. If any key data field does not have data, the analysis will not be able to do.

- Effectiveness

  - All data collected should be within normal range
    or have a minimum range of exceptional cases.
    The surface quality of steel plates is closely related
    to the operational metrics of the milling machine,
    for instance speed, pressure, or temperature. Each
    metric has a value within the allowable range.
    Sometimes, it marks exceptionally and temporarily
    high speed than design tolerance, but it does not
    make sense if the device detects outliers
    consistently.

- Accuracy

  - Accuracy is directly related to the reliability of
    data. If the data does not have enough levels of
    accuracy, the analysis does not return any
    meaningful results. For instance, a consultant
    wants to analyze the overdue account receivable
    by product and region. If a currency rate was not
    correctly applied, it is also inaccurate when they
    confirm the overdue of the account receivable.

- Integrity

  - It is the key criteria to make sure that the data is
    not redundantly organized and meets mutually
    exclusive collectively exhaustive. Consultant tries
    to pull out financial report after consolidating the

financial report of an overseas entity. If both entities have a significantly different scheme of chart of account, the consolidated report does not present data integrity.

Organize data

Data is a set of values of subjects for qualitative or quantitative variables. When data is processed, organized, structured, or presented in a given context to make the value, it is called information. Data organization is the practice of categorizing and classifying data to make it more usable. Like maintaining documents in the file folder, a consultant arranges gathered data in the most logical and orderly manner. It can be categorized as structured, unstructured, or semi-structured data according to the data scheme.

When gathering data, a consultant can use several tools, such as surveys, focus groups, interviews, and questionnaires. To help organize data, a consultant can use charts and graphs to help visualize what's going on, such as bar graphs, frequency charts, picture graphs, and line graphs. If the data is gathered not for statistical analysis, a consultant considers organizing the data upon the pattern. Several examples of patterns below are valuable to organize qualitative or unstructured data.

- Chronological Patterns
  Example) Year of Publication[25]

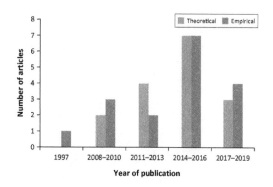

- Spatial Patterns
  Example) Oil and Gas Pipelines[26]

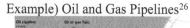

---

[25] https://www.researchgate.net/
[26] Map by Virginia W. Mason, National Geographic

- Sequential Patterns
    Example) Year of Publication[27]

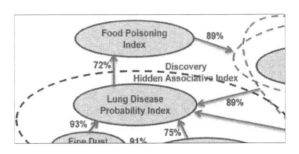

- Compare-Contrast Patterns
    Example) Compare vs. Contrast[28]

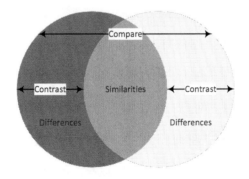

---

[27] https://www.researchgate.net/
[28] https://misusedword.weebly.com/

- Cause-Effect Patterns
  Example[29]

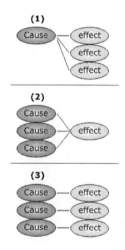

- Topical Patterns
  Example) Types of Wine

  - Red wines
    - European
      - Bordeaux
      - Burgundy
    - Californian
      - Cabernet
      - Sauvignon

---

[29] https://www.rit.edu/

- White wines
  - European
    - Bordeaux
    - Mosel
  - Californian
    - Sauvignon Blanc
    - Chardonnay

Progress sharing

Typically, the client does want to get the progress of each task, review the facts with implications, provide input, and articulate direction upon their priority. A consultant keeps independency against any inappropriate influence from key stakeholders. But, at the same time, a consultant needs to keep communicating the status upon facts in transparently. A consultant needs to make the session as a momentum of change management, build consensus, promote business awareness for assessment, approve the status with the next step, and bring management sponsorship.

Below lists the key skeleton of progress sharing when a consultant plans communication protocol and delivers progress updates over the project term.

Timing or cadence of progress sharing
- Regular meeting cadence
  - Daily, Weekly, Bi-weekly, Monthly

- Report-out session upon event
  - Customer survey, workshop, statistical analysis, voice of customer

- Official sign-off session
  - Kick-off, interim report-out session, mid-term report, final report

Key agenda of progress sharing session

- Observations, fact findings with implications
- Hypothesis and test results
- Problem and causes
- Awareness or feedback of key stakeholders
- Current accomplishment of key measures, benchmarks
- Criteria to decide on a priority
- Initiatives with a priority
- Risk exposures and mitigation
- Justification and rationale
- Key decision item to move toward next steps

Target audiences

- Key decision maker
  - Executive leadership or board of directors
  - Project champion
- Promoting party
  - Process owner

- Functional leadership
- External key stakeholder
  - Customer
  - Strategic investor or financial investor

Protocol of session

- Public hearing
- Presentation and Q&A session
- Round table for open discussion
- Workshop
- Symposium
- Newsletter, billboard, magazine, podcast

2.3 Action planning

Everyone will recognize Benz as the best premium brand, but considering its performance, Benz is a car that requires a lot of maintenance. Therefore, it is necessary to select a vehicle suitable for an individual by considering various factors such as operation cost, residual value, and image according to vehicle ownership. Likewise, while there are similarities in choosing a solution to an alternative to a problem, there are also many differences because a client has typically unique challenges. That means the best solution for the client may not be the best solution for another client.

Action planning is a process of developing a solution to the problem analyzed in the diagnosis stage. It includes a process of deriving and selecting alternatives. Since action planning is developed based on the analysis of a problem comparing objectives, it is important to make sure the problems defined are critical issues when considering the client's aspirations with objectives. In other words, a future direction should be addressed to resolve a problem aligned with the client's business priorities and drive changes to improve the business processes going towards a vision. Also, it is a task to present the action plan to the client and prepare the implementation of the solution selected by the client.

The action plan establishment stage requires an approach based on innovation and creativity rather than an analytical approach such as the diagnosis stage. This step is not about getting additional data or explanations for an existing problem, it's about discovering something new to resolve the problem. Although the solutions that the consultant provides to clients do not always contain new ideas, it is often a mistake in the consulting process to apply common solutions as a practice that does not consider the unique problems of the clients.

Ideation

The client expects the consultant to present the optimal solution or opportunity to the company, but it is not easy to get an optimal solution immediately. For clients, since most problems have a complex relationship between cause and effect, numerous solutions and combinations of these alternatives are often discussed, and there are cases in which it is difficult to distinguish the priorities clearly between them.

Action planning begins with generating ideas to develop a solution for problems defined. The solution must address the nature of the problem, domain practices, and complexity of the problem. Idea generation is one side of the ideation process, and it gets improved based on the feedback from the idea evaluation. So, the ideation requires an iterative process till the idea meets a requirement achieved.[30]

---

[30] https://nesslabs.com/idea-evaluation

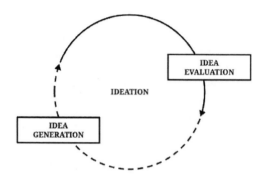

- Idea generation. The phase of the creative process is about coming up with many blind variations to solve a problem. Quantity is the measure of performance.
- Idea evaluation. In this phase, selective judgment is applied by assessing how practical, useful, or relevant each idea is. The goal is to keep quality ideas only.

"Idea generation could be thought of as a search for novelty, while its process partner, idea evaluation, might be thought of as an effort to make novel thinking practical, useful or relevant." – Gerard Puccio and John Cabra[31].

Idea generation

---

[31] Organizational Creativity: A Practical Guide for Innovators & Entrepreneurs

Below are listed several well-known techniques promoting idea generation when a consultant gets it drafted.

- Mind mapping

  - It is useful when presenting data visually. Also, it drives idea generation upon several dimensions defined. The template below[32] tells several ideas with supporting ideas to resolve the subject or objectives. Each idea should be exclusive to the other, and the supporting evidence is also exclusively defined under the idea. It is similar to the issue tree that a consultant has utilized for clarifying root causes.

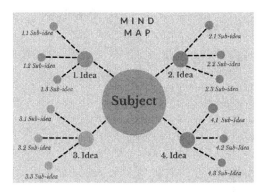

---

[32] https://www.lawpracticetoday.org/

- Reverse thinking

    - This technique makes a consultant think in another way. For example, a client wants to know "how to increase the number of members of your business". According to this technique, a consultant should think "how can the company not increase its membership?". To this question, some clients may look for an answer by not improving service quality or reducing benefits, etc. Those answers will be reversed and converted to the idea to resolve the problems defined. This idea generation technique works for the concept that it's easier to come up with negative suggestions.

- Brainstorming

    - It is a group creativity technique that brings many ideas out. It is useful when a group needs to generate plenty of ideas within a limited time, and it is not a matter of the quality of an idea. People can think without restrictions, and they suggest as many spontaneous new ideas as possible. All the ideas are noted down without criticism, and the ideas are evaluated after the brainstorming session.

- SCAMPER[33]

---

[33] SCAMPER was proposed by Alex Faickney Osborn in 1953 and was

- The word SCAMPER is an acronym and an activity-based thought process that can be performed by cooperative learning. Typically, a consultant supports clients in selecting a particular topic and helps them to develop it through a structured process. Each part of the acronym helps us think and ask questions, which brings the idea generation.
    - [S] Substitute; Comes up with another item that is equivalent to the topic
    - [C] Combine; Adds information to the original topic
    - [A] Adapt; Adjusts and identifies ways to construct the topic
    - [M] Modify; Magnify, minify changes the topic creatively
    - [P] Put; Put possible scenarios and situations where the topic applied
    - [E] Eliminate; Remove ideas from the topic that is not valuable
    - [R] Reverse; Rearrange or evolves a new concept from the original concept
- For example, if a client who owns a contact center business wants to reduce call waiting time in the rush window, a consultant may think self-service, artificial intelligence-based chatbot as a 'substitute' instead of adding call center agents during the peak time.

---

further developed by Bob Eberle in 1971 in his book 'SCAMPER: Games for Imagination Development'.

- Storyboarding

  - This technique refers to the process of making storyboards to generate ideas. Storyboards use pictures, illustrations, and other information to present the ideas better way. For example, suppose a consultant is working on an idea for a private banker. A consultant can portray the different scenes in the form of a storyboard starting from reaching the sales lead as a moment of truth. This helps you in better visualization and you can make changes accordingly.
  - Example: Lost report

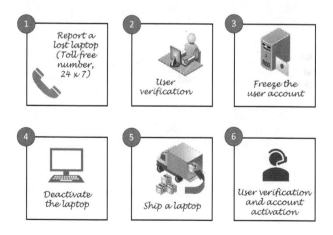

- Role-Playing

  - In this technique, the participants take up roles to play. These roles are different from the ones they usually play. It adds an element of fun and helps get innovative ideas. For example, a consultant can take up the roles of the black consumer and discuss their behavior with expectations. This could lead a group to stumble upon some good ideas.

- Brainwriting

  - A group of people writes their ideas on paper. After a certain designated time, the chairman reads the idea and adds another idea to the paper. It is for elaborating supporting ideas or promoting another idea. This continues until everyone has put their idea on paper. Upon this approach, there will be a discussion on each aspect by all stakeholders.
  - A consultant can develop and apply their template to the topic, but below presents one of the famous toolkits to promote brainwriting on the website[34].

---

[34] https://conceptboard.com/

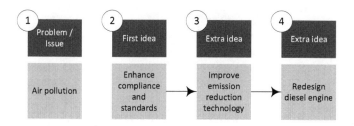

- Forced Relationship

    - This technique helps to come up with unique ideas. Here you take two unrelated things and imagine putting them together to see what new thing you can come up with. For example, a baby stroller and a golf bag seem like items that are unrelated to each other. Now try putting them together. You might get an interesting idea for target segmentation like a van or SUV which has enough space to load luggage as a second car for a family that has recently infant.

- The 5 W's

    - Who, What, Where, When, and Why.
    - Answering these five W makes accomplish a multi-dimensional perspective of the topic under discussion and is an efficient way to come up with solutions and ideas.
    - For example, suppose the client wants to introduce

a new model in country A. Based on the market survey, a consultant needs to drive discussion for 5Ws.

Knowledge management

A consultant can discover and utilize knowledge as an asset while developing alternatives to resolve the challenges under objectives. The followings are examples of assets that will be maintained and utilized for consultancy services.

- Industry standard framework
- Industry benchmarks
- Articles in a journal, magazine, conference, newspaper
- White paper published by the government, international organizations
- Sanitized report of another client's project
- Standard process or platform
- Market data
- Subject Matter Expert's experiences

The advantages when a consultant utilizes knowledge assets would be categorized as below.

- Qualified approach according to reality in an effective and efficient manner

- Credible reference makes risk exposures minimizing or preventing in advance
- Easy to build consensus and moderate interest conflicts

At the same time, there should be disadvantages when a consultant sticks to applying or counting on knowledge assets too much.

- Lack of differentiation or down leveling brought by unconditional adoption of the asset
- Stereotypes brings not to make thinking out of the box unless a consultant fully understands the implications of the knowledge assets
- Resource consumption in an inefficient way when a consultant is not familiar with the case or does not have knowledge of how to use the assets

Knowledge management is the most popular agenda which has been discussed to leverage the asset within consulting services industry in an effective way. As we've briefly listed above, consultancy tries to maximize asset utilization and minimize poor quality at the same time. Many empirical studies have been discovered to improve effectiveness while consultant utilizes knowledge asset, and the research[35] below tells key interests with strategy when consultancy maintains knowledge assets.

---

[35] Morten T. Hansen, Nitin Nohria, and Thomas J. Tierney., "What is your strategy for managing knowledge?", Harvard Business Review, Mar-Apr, 1999

How Consulting Firms Manage Their Knowledge		
CODIFICATION Provide high-quality, reliable, and fast information systems implementation by reusing codified knowledge.	Competitive Strategy	Personalization Provide creative, analytically rigorous advice on high-level strategic problems by channeling individual expertise.
REUSE ECONOMICS: Invest once in a knowledge asset; reuse it many times Use large teams with a high ratio of associates to partners Focus on generating large overall revenues	Economic Model	EXPERT ECONOMICS: Charge high fees for highly customized solutions to unique problems Use small teams with a low ratio of associates to partners
PEOPLE-TO-DOCUMENTS: Develop an electronic document system that codifies, stores, disseminates, and allows reuse of knowledge	Knowledge Management Strategy	PERSON-TO-PERSON Develop networks for linking people so that tacit knowledge can be shared
Invest heavily in IT: The goal is to connect people with reusable codified knowledge	Information Technology	Invest moderately in IT: The goal is to facilitate conversations and the exchange of tacit knowledge
Hire new college graduates who are well suited to the reuse of knowledge and the implementation of solutions Train people in groups and through computer-based distance learning Reward people for using and contributing to document databases	Human Resources	Hire MBAs who like problem solving and can tolerate ambiguity Train people through one-on-one mentoring Reward people for direct sharing knowledge with others
Earnst & Young	Examples	McKinsey & Co.

Develop resolution or alternative

Based on the study or assessment for As-Is, a consultant is looking for future directions with resolutions to address problems or challenges. Also, the resolution should be aligned with the client's business objectives and priorities. For developing the solution, a consultant utilizes various techniques to generate ideas or get inspired by leveraging knowledge assets as proven references.

Although a consultant and key stakeholders within the client might have a common consensus for challenges, problems, and root causes at the assessment stage, it is natural to compare and compete with different solutions to the same root causes. For productive discussion, a consultant needs to promote the client makes clarify and describe more details of solutions.

Case) One for all, All for one.

Company X produces construction equipment and sells it through a franchise dealership channel. They are making 20+ products of six product groups at five production sites in three countries across the world.

Typically, the construction equipment industry has an economic cycle every decade upon housing economy or social infrastructure investment. When local government or municipal agency initiates multi-year projects such as highway, bridge, and school construction, it brings sales opportunities to company X regardless of procurement or lease. Typically, each project requires at least 36 months for implementation, and the buyer is very sensitive to the interest rates and the future economy after the project.

Besides, construction equipment consumes a mass amount of fossil fuel and brings air pollution, and the government keeps enhancing regulations to reduce carbon emissions. Their brand aims at mid-tier products, not for the premier customer or price-sensitive customers; however, it has made their brand awareness an ambiguous position in the market. With these rationales, many buyers prefer to buy an equipment machine under the considerations of upfront cost, regular operation cost, and residual value.

For instance, the premier customer is usually sensitive to non-price factors such as maintenance support, reliability, durability, and residual value when they sell it out after 48 months. For the same product, the self-employed customer is looking for financing conditions, upfront costs, and maintenance costs.

According to the market survey what they have done in the assessment, company X has a poor market share compared with its competitors for the last three years. Also, their profitability has been got worse over the years as the sales team has driven market penetration upon deep discount offers. Besides, they are told the government considers announcing more strict regulations for customer rights, and it will bring additional quality costs as a contingency in case of a voluntary recall. At the same time, company X has to build and maintain a quality assurance process that requires huge investment with ongoing operating costs.

Key stakeholders and a consultant had several rounds of a workshop to develop resolutions for getting market share, improving profitability, and customer retention. Their expected window is limited to the next coming three years, and there are several restrictions such as resources, budget, knowledge, and experiences that are not able to get internalized immediately.

When the consultant has a roundtable with dealer management, they pointed price is not attractive compared with competitors and emphasized company X needs to provide further channel discounts for a dealership to encourage sales. They've urged non-financial benefits such as an extended warranty, trade-in value, or subsidy for dealer sales as non-financial benefits if company X does not want to provide deep discounts.

In another case, engineering leadership is concerned with product strategy instead of sales promotion and highlights quality improvement as the only effective solution to improve brand value. They've pointed out that residual value is significantly lower than a competitor for over 48 months old machines in the market. As a result, it has brought a relatively higher amount of upfront cost as well as monthly recurring cost if the customer buys it with financing.

At the same time, sales operation has emphasized that market share is closely related to machine availability when a dealership looks for a machine. To improve machine availability, company X needs to increase inventory and make more additional yards. Unfortunately, it hits operating capital and an overhead cost if the count of an aged machine keeps growing. Also, it brings negative value to the financial book as a result.

All key stakeholders are aware of the poor loyalty of their brand in the market and regard it as an opportunity for the next three years. As per the root cause, most stakeholders have pointed out poor quality experiences comparing price conditions in the market. However, they faced the challenge of selecting what solution will be an effective alternative to improve it. Unfortunately, the management leadership of company X knows they have other business priorities for the next three years and believe they do not have an internal capability to develop/implement the changes.

Each stakeholder has pointed out the root cause as well as a resolution by each function correctly and respectively. As a consultant, what should be the best idea to moderate and bring the best solution out of various candidates? Stakeholder tends to reverse the discrimination in some cases if their initiative is not selected after reprioritization according to the reports. What should be the common criteria to decide? What procedure will be applicable to select the initiative? How can make key stakeholders make their commitment to the corporate agenda? What governance will make initiatives implementation and operation as planned? Any compensation or promotion to encourage active engagement?

Validate the initiative candidates

When a consultant gathers resolution candidates from each stakeholder, they should assess and verify the effectiveness of a resolution candidate when a client implements it. Assessment criteria will be usually developed by a consultant, confirmed by the client, assessed by commissioners, and approved by management executives. Below tells common criteria of assessment with quantified metrics as an example.

Completeness	<ul><li>Details of what to do and how to do</li><li>Alignment with priorities</li><li>Fitness with objectives</li><li>Business justifications</li><li>Roles and responsibilities</li><li>Timeline</li><li>Budget projection</li><li>Financing strategy</li></ul>
Readiness	<ul><li>Technical feasibility</li><li>Organizational readiness</li><li>Market maturity</li><li>Regulation or compliance</li><li>Resource availability</li></ul>

	• Change readiness

Financial Justification	• Break-even analysis • Contribution margin review • Internal rate of return • Return on investment • Free cash flow • Total cost of ownership

Governance	• Definition of success • Acceptance criteria • Threshold • Escalation process upon event • Risk exposure and mitigation

Although quantified factors will not be able to validate resolution candidates in a case, a consultant needs to do their best effort validates initiatives with quantitative measures. In many cases, it is really hard to justify or validate value when the opportunity is associated with ethics, morale, satisfaction, training, or fundamentals of operation.

For instance, the quality tracking and reporting process would be a good tool to keep and track quality inspection by procedures. Also, quality tracking will be able to provide evidence when they get an audit from external appraisers. However, it is typically hard to justify the benefits in monetary value when a client implements the quality tracking process, and they will emphasize that it is a kind of fundamental process running with overhead cost. Unfortunately, the back-office function has similar challenges when they review the opportunities.

For making better verification of opportunities for the back-office, a consultant usually assesses it with the respect to an opportunity loss. Opportunity loss tells the monetary value of risk exposure which should be brought by not implementing the opportunity in the near future. In general, opportunity lost is calculated upon the probability of event times the expected losses. If company X does not have a quality tracking process, it may or may not be bringing negative financial impacts such as recall, payment associated with settlements, or court-ordered judgment according to product liability, etc. Likewise, IT security is also one of the areas that should be reviewed and verified under the consideration of opportunity lost instead of financial benefits.

Case) Do it now or later.

☐ Do it now
or
☑ Make it later

Company Y has recently acquired Company Z to gain more market share in the industry. Company Y produces industrial equipment for road construction, and Company Z sells common consumable goods for the industrial equipment industry. Management of company Y believes they will be able to do more business by consolidating business with Company Zs and want to merge both companies reasonably.

The revenue and asset value of Company Z is approximately half of Company Y as the unit price of a product is cheaper than company Y. However, Company Z has reported EBIT[36] as almost two times greater than Company Y because Company Z does not have aged inventory or overdue account receivables. As a result, Company Z was able to reduce the contingency to the minimum level in its annual report.

The business of both companies is heavily dependent on infrastructure projects such as road construction, building a bridge, tunnel construction, etc. Usually, the project runs for at least three to five years, and the local government prefers to make a contract with a sole vendor by consolidating various subcontractors to simplify vendor management.

Management of Company Y has asked to draft a business consolidation strategy and also identified several guidelines as thresholds below when they decide and approve the consolidation plan later.
> 1) Not allowed to hire resources except backfill
> 2) Maintain the same or achieve greater EBIT during the transition
> 3) Need to realize business synergy.

---

[36] EBIT, Earning Before Income Tax

Strategy leadership has started a project for consolidation strategy with the assistance of consultancy services. They've picked up talents from both companies and mobilized the project team. The talent represents several key business lines such as pricing, production, procurement, engineering, dealer management, services, accounting, human resources, and sales operation. The team has assessed the existing capabilities of both companies and developed consolidation strategies with opportunities. Also, the consultancy has provided market dynamics and practices as a reference, and management studies carefully the implications of each reference.

One of the priorities is to decide the right level of integration of both companies in three years. In case of a market-facing process, all business stakeholder wants to run the business separately not to lose their customer base and keep their brand value. At the same time, the back-office function prefers to consolidate both business operations quickly in a significant way to realize cost saving earlier. The accounting team analyzes and compares SG&A[37] costs of both businesses; however, they know it has a series of prerequisites such as standardizing the chart of account. Also, the HR team is eager to mobilize the talent of both companies instead of hiring new employees from the market. To promote and mobilize talent, they need to set criteria to assess the capabilities

[37] Selling General & Administrative Expense, SG&A)

of candidates. It does mean that it requires huge amounts of investment with efforts to realize synergy.

For those reasons, sales operation is looking for an opportunity to share and utilize available occupancy at the warehouse of each end instead of getting another new occupancy contracting. Unfortunately, the product of both companies has far different dimension from each other for delivery, repairs, and maintenance. Company Y produces their product starting from at least 10 tonnage weight with 10-foot height. As a result, their dealership has a tall ceiling at their workshop. Company Z their product is more likely a cubical box to deliver disposable goods under limited space. For instance, an air filter has around 10 pounds weight at most and is easy to load on the deck. In another business case, they try to make a bundled offer by combining products of each end such as products with annual MRO[38] services.

One of the opportunities has a strong justification for the expected benefit if company Y implements it regardless of poor return on the investment. The other opportunity can propose a pretty much clearly defined cost, but it is not easy to project the return in monetary value. Another opportunity is regarded as a fundamental initiative of all other opportunities even the opportunity itself does not return any direct benefit.

As a consultant, how to drive discussion and moderate

---

[38] Maintenance, Repair, and Operation

conflicts of interest among stakeholders under the defined criteria? Any idea to make opportunities for candidate prioritization do you have?

Assess initiative candidates

Typically, stakeholders have an internal consensus for the evaluation criteria to decide the priority among opportunities. Effectiveness, efficiency, feasibility, low risk, return on investment, and regulation will be the most popular criteria. However, it has competing concerns when stakeholders discuss the weight of each decision criteria. For instance, qualitative initiatives will be able to get intangible benefits instead of expected returns. The technical initiatives will be easily justified feasibility, although there should be a different level of acceptable risk by stakeholders.

A consultant needs to have an in-depth discussion with the key decision makers in advance to get their intention about the weight among the factors of evaluation criteria. If management leadership wants to transform the existing operating model fundamentally for cost rationalization, the level of standardization may be defined as one of the key factors.

At the organization, a consultant needs to understand the overall acceptance of the changes within the client's organization. Some client does want to move quickly and aggressively despite taking risks. For the same condition, other clients may want to accept and implement the change upon the other's qualified reference. For the same matter, another client prefers a deployment upon pilot implementation. The other client may prefer to convert all the domains at one time immediately to drive the change radically. A consultant needs to understand key stakeholders' preferences while they have an initial meeting before beginning the project.

For example, company B considers new business on top of the existing line of business. The new business requires huge investment for the next three years. Also, they are told that their industry has uncertainties brought by technological convergence. As a result, they are expecting to see an industry downturn and strong growth at the same possibility within three to five years. Upon their market research, the team reported below.

- Option 1. Aggressively drives new business with huge investment
- Option 2. Drives new business, but invests upon returns over the next three years
  - Option 3. Implement new business for pilot only. Once confirm the business model, will decide the next step to deploy it

Candidate	Opportunity 1	Opportunity 2	Opportunity 3
Strong growth	$190M	$40M	$60M
Industry downturn	($30M)	$10M	$50M

While assessing the initiatives with the priority will be different upon the risk profile of a decision maker.

At MaxMin

- Select candidates from the most conservative & passive scenarios.
- Take the most positive solution out of the candidate selected.
- With this principle, ($30M) of option 1, $10M of option 2, and $50M of option 3 are listed, and a decision maker prefers to take option 3.

At MiniMax

- Select candidates from the most positive & active projection.
- Take the most conservative solution out of the candidate selected.
- Under this principle, $190M of option 1, $40M of option 2, and $60M of option 3 are listed, and a decision maker takes option 2.

At MaxMax

- Select candidates from the most positive & active projection.
- Take the most positive and aggressive solution out of

the candidate selected. It should be the most aggressive option but should be at high risk in other words.

- For these criteria, a decision maker takes option 1.

At MiniMini

- Select candidates from the most passive & conservative projections.
- Take the most conservative one out of the candidate selected.
- At these criteria, a decision maker takes option 2.

The above four principles are simplified illustrations to help everyone's understanding. While the consultant prioritizes the options, there are usually complicated criteria that require a qualitative judgment to make a better decision instead of taking the initiative emotionally or intuitively. Below tells a couple of decision criteria under moderating risk exposure.

- Savage's criterion

  - It advises taking an opportunity upon an expected tradeoff or regrets.
  - A decision maker assumes that a tradeoff or regrets are closely related to an expected value of the opportunity, and they need to understand the tradeoff or regrets that will be affected by scenarios. Select the option which has the most minimum levels of regrets out of candidates which has a bigger tradeoff or regrets.
  - The approach will make a more rationalized

comparison among scenarios under the expected impact. However, there is a possibility to take the most exceptional cases if the projection is a bit extremely contrasted. Although opportunity "1" is selected upon Savage's criterion, it will be the less preferred option compared to other options in common sense. So, a consultant needs to review and validate the expected return with regrets by each projection.

- Under this approach, opportunity "1" is selected.

Candidate	Opportunity 1	Opportunity 2	Opportunity 3
Strong growth	$190M	$40M	$60M
Industry downturn	($30M)	$10M	$50M
Regret under strong growth	$190M - $190M = 0	$190M - $40M = $150M	$190M - $60M = $130M
Regret under industry downturn	$50M – ($30M) = $80M	$50M - $10M = $40M	$50M - $50M = 0
Regret at minimum out of regret at maximum	$80M	$150M	$130M

- Decision under risk

  - Apply the degree of optimism (or called the possibility to happen the event) of each case and calculate a final score. For instance, if SME[39] estimates strong growth for the next several years and judges 70% of the possibilities for the scenario above, 70% is applied to the degree of optimism. In other words, 30% will be for the possibility of an industry downturn. The sum of possibility should be the same as 100%.

- It gives a more balanced approach to projected possibilities of events. However, it has a bit of risk or bias that may be associated with subjectiveness when the SME forecasts the event upon their judgment. Under this approach, opportunity 3 is selected.

Candidate	Opportunity 1	Opportunity 2	Opportunity 3
Strong growth	$190M	$40M	$60M
Industry downturn	($30M)	$10M	$50M
Strong growth with the degree of optimism	$190M × 0.7 = $133M	$40M × 0.7 = $28M	$60M × 0.7 = $42M
Industry downturn with the degree of optimism	($30M) × 0.3 = ($90M)	$10M × 0.3 = $3M	$50M × 0.3 = $15M
Weighted value	$43M	$31M	$57M

- Decision tree

    - Under the assumption that an event or given

---

[39] Subject Matter Expert

conditions bring another event out, a consultant develops a decision alternative by elaborating on an event. Each decision alternative has a degree of optimism set with a projection of return. Each possibility is typically generated by a moderated discussion among the subject matter experts such as the Delphi method.

- Due to the driven event upon the predecessor, it has a structural dependence among events. It does mean that a wrong event with estimated possibilities makes the rest of the events ineffectively. It effectively fits well with the decision agenda when it requires conditional judgment under multiple variables. Statistically, it is the same as Bayesian statistics[40] and like AHP[41].

---

[40] Introduced by Thomas Bayes based on the Bayesian theorem in 1763.
[41] Analytic Hierarchy Process, Developed by Thomas L. Saaty, in 1970s.

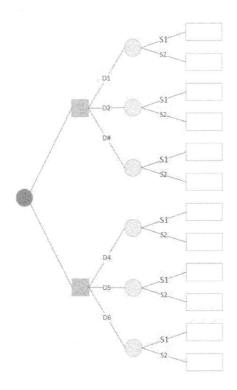

Draft an implementation plan

An implementation plan describes the detail of each initiative by the defined phases. What, when, how, why, prerequisites, interdependency, and acceptance criteria may be an example of the details of an initiative. Although the initiatives have been validated when a consultant has developed them, they cannot work well without an implementation plan. So, implementation planning is much more important than any other phase of a consulting project to make the initiative effective.

Implementation planning typically starts with considering the available resources of the client. Resources include talent, time, budget, physical occupancy, license, goodwill, royalty, sales channel, logistics, etc. At the same time, a consultant needs to exchange an initial thought with a client for the scope, phase, and target value to achieve after implementation.

Although there was a task to confirm the priorities among initiatives when they verify alternatives, a consultant needs to revisit it with a client. For instance, there should be a different preference for the priorities when a client drafts an implementation plan. Sometimes, they compare seriously the expected return when the initiative is implemented. It may be associated with the cultural backgrounds or personal experiences of the decision maker.

Case) Which one is better than others?

Company ABC has twenty sites in the UK, India, Korea, and the USA. One of the most advanced production sites is located in the USA, and they produce approximately a quarter of the whole unit of the company ABC makes it across the world. USA facility is ten times bigger than a site in India and has the most complicated process for most of the product line.

Some decision-makers believe that they need to start implementation from the Indian site as it has relatively easy to implement than the USA site. It does mean that they can manage and control. Although it may be hard to improve the performance significantly, it can recover when the issue hits on.

On the other hands, some other key stakeholders have a little different position. They want to implement the initiative at the USA site as it has most of the processes and practices that company ABC has in twenty sites across the world. It does mean that they believe they can implement most of the improvement at once when they complete it on the USA site. Also, they think it is effective and can promote change management. It will be a great success when they implement the initiative within budget within a timeline with manageable risks. If not, it will bring tons of impact to business operation and makes negative perception against changes.

Which approach will be more effective than the other?

In other cases, a client prefers to implement the change initiatives by a spiral approach which is the implementation iteratively. It moderates conflict interests among stakeholders and makes priority under the pros and cons. Once the scope, phase, task, deliverables, duration, acceptance criteria, champion, and required capabilities are defined, a consultant should validate it again under the defined objectives of an implementation plan. Timeline and budget are key components when a consultant develops the implementation plan.

Usually, a consultant utilizes several tools to make working more efficient when developing and wrapping up the plan. Microsoft Project is well-known software when a consultant develops a schedule, resources, and budgets by task. It also can simulate workload over the whole implementation plan. The software provides benefits by running CPM[42] with PERT[43] to verify the project plan from beginning to end.

For instance, it seems like task #7 is regarded as one of the bottlenecks to forward task #8 in the diagram below. However, #2 task and #4 are positioned as a burden when we consider predecessors of each. Upon the CPM chart below, 14 weeks is estimated from tasks #1 thru #4 to #7. Consultant needs to verify the task with conditions and may need to consider adding more resources/budget into task #2 or reroute the task upon redefined other tasks.

If a client does not have available resources or budget to expedite the task, a consultant may need to recommend or propose splitting the plan into several phases if a client does agree to revise their target to improve.

---

[42] Critical Path Method
[43] Program Evaluation and Review Technique

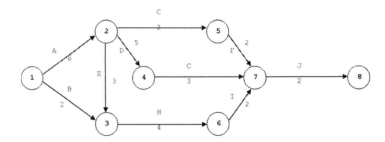

During these planning processes, a consultant should make a client engage in every step when it requires a business decision. Typically, business wants to involve and influence their expectation in the implementation plan as it is directly tied to their MBO[44] and their incentive scheme as well. If a key business owner thinks that the initiatives or changes affect a negative impact on the business operation, they will not be engaged proactively while implementing the initiatives. In other words, they will respond passively or do not provide their commitment, and it should be a critically negative influence for driving changes across the organization. However, a consultant needs to understand the objectives of implementation and tries to avoid any compromise against the objectives.

Key components of the implementation plan will be typically as below.

- Initiative definition includes acceptance criteria
- Required budget, skillset, and resources for each

---

[44] Management By Objectives

initiative
- Risk identified and mitigation
- Change management
- Program management
- Communication and escalation

One of the most important pieces of the implementation plan should be the change management over the whole change process. Implementation planning requires drafting action items upon investigation based on reality under desires. However, change management requires realizing the action item responsively. For change management, it will be described in more detail in chapter 3 later.

Report-out to key stakeholders and get the buy-in decision

As part of the officialization process, a consultant prepares a report-out session to get buy-in decisions from the key business stakeholders. Typically, it is for delivering change direction with a key theme to the stakeholders who will have to get the change. While designing the session, a consultant needs to consider the overall scenario according to the objectives and critical success factors of an implementation plan. To set the report-out strategy, a consultant needs to discuss and promotes to build consensus with a client in advance.

- Objectives of the report-out session

- Key theme to deliver
- Key takeaway or expected challenges from stakeholders
- Attendees
- Speakers

The skeleton of the report-out session will be drafted as an example below although a consultant needs to adjust the balance or sequence of deliverables to align expectations with key stakeholders.

- Objectives of the consulting project

  - Key findings with implications of As-Is study
  - Key challenges
  - Market dynamics and implications

- Key opportunities

  - Justifications with rationale
  - Prioritize initiatives and change direction
  - Expected benefits

- Implementation plan

  - Project management
  - Organization
  - Budget
  - Required capabilities

- Resource plan

• Risk and mitigation

- Change management
- Communication and escalation

At the same time, it is also important to decide on attendees of the report-out session when a consultant drafts the objectives of a session. Usually, a consultant has close communication with key stakeholders in advance and has a chance to build a consensus for the decisions before the session. So, it does not make sense to bring an open item to the table if there is a significantly different concern against the decision because the report-out session would not be a session for brainstorming to elaborate on an open discussion.

Selecting attendees would be an important item that aligns with the protocol of the report-out session. If it requires an official approval to change direction with investment, the attendees may be selected from the member of the board of directors. If the session is designed to get a commitment from each process owner, a consultant considers functional leaders of both organizations as attendees. If the opportunity brings cultural changes across the company, a client should appoint employees by each function or level as attendees. In the same matter, key customers or suppliers will be invited as an audience, if the change requires active engagement while a client implements the opportunities.

In the same manner, the consultant should decide on a

presentation strategy such as who will lead a presentation. If management leaders prefer to get in-depth knowledge from the report-out session, a consultant may be the right person to drive the session. In other cases, key business leaders will be the main attendee if the decision maker wants to endorse a sponsorship with commitment. For the specific area, a consultant may delegate key business stakeholders makes key attendees select.

In detail, there will be more technical questions such as whether assign a speaker by topic or make a head speaker presents all topics. Also, the Q&A session strategy will be one of the parties to designing the presentation scenario. Other protocols such as seat assignment for offline attendees, online meeting setup, preparing a leaflet, drafting/distributing a minute, and key speech of business leaders should be decided in alignment with the objectives of a session.

A consultant and a client need to be aware that the implementation plan will be activated when it is officially approved by key stakeholders, committed by key business leaders, and sponsored by business ownership. Below tells several Do's and Don'ts while delivering a presentation.

- Do's

    - Delivers at stakeholders' point of view
    - Highlights why and what
    - Appeals business justification aligned with business objectives
    - Emphasizes benefits as well as risks
    - Explains opportunities over the cross-functional

process
- Be glad to get feedback from attendees

- Don'ts

  - Not stick to technical capabilities only
  - Not to explain too many details about how
  - Not to react against challenges raised by attendees immediately
  - Not make an improvised decision according to a response from attendees
  - Not compromise with stakeholders' interest
  - Not commit or accept every requirement, but classify it for the next step

2.4 Implementation

Project Management

Key features of the project

The Project Management Institute[45] defines a 'project as a temporary endeavor undertaken to create a unique product, service or result.' It may be executed individually or collaboratively and involved in the research that plans to achieve a particular aim. An alternative sees a project managerially as a sequence of events: a 'set of interrelated tasks to be executed over a fixed period and within certain cost and other limitations.'

The word 'temporary' means projects must have a defined beginning and end, and every project must include a timeline, scope, and resources. It has a clearly defined set of targets or objectives to sort out business challenges under given conditions. It means a project is not part of ongoing regular operations. It tells a project is a means to respond to the demand that cannot be addressed within the client's normal operational limits. Projects are critical to implementing the client's business strategy, and examples of projects are as below[46].

---

[45] https//www.project manageri.org
[46] A Guide to the Project Management Body of Knowledge (PMBOK

- Developing a new product or services
- Effecting a change in structure, staffing, or style of an organization
- Designing a new transportation equipment
- Developing or acquiring a new or modified information system
- Implementing a new business procedure or process

A project is usually defined as a group of opportunities, and the project can be managed under a program if a client has multiple projects.

Definition of project management

Project management is the organization of knowledge, skills, tools, and techniques to project activities to meet project requirements. Project management is accomplished through the use of the five processes such like initiating, planning, executing, monitoring & controlling, and closing. The project team manages the work of projects, and the work typically involves below.

- Competing demands for scope, time, cost, risk, and quality
- Stakeholders with differing needs and expectations

Guide, 2000 Edition)

- Identified requirements

Project management process

One of the well-known project management processes developed by the Project Management Institute has five groups of the process as below. The process group does not walk like a waterfall, and it interacts with the prior process group upon the validation. Project Management Process has a long history with academic research since last 50 years to make a project accomplish objectives and improve the quality of project deliverables. It is a completely separate domain of this book, and we just wanted to walk through key features with implications of the process instead of the process itself. We cite key definitions from PMBOK Guide below.

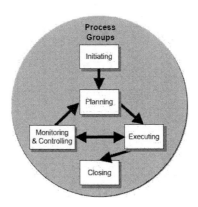

- Initiating processes-authorizing the project or phase.
- Planning processes-defining and refining objectives and selecting the best action or alternative to attain the objectives that the project was undertaken to address.
- Executing processes-coordinating people and other resources to carry out the plan.
- Controlling processes-ensuring that project objectives are met by monitoring and measuring progress regularly to identify variances from the plan so that corrective action can be taken when necessary.
- Closing processes-formalizing acceptance of the project or phase and bringing it to an orderly end.

These five process groups require capabilities with the knowledge to run the process correctly. At the same time, it can be categorized knowledge area across process groups as below[47].
It states that this table is not meant to be exclusive, but to indicate generally where the project management processes fit into both the project management process groups and the project management knowledge areas. Below tells planning, executing, and controlling of whole processes.

	Planning	Executing	Controlling
Integration Management	Project Plan Development	Project Plan Execution	Integrated Change Control
Scope Management	Scope Planning Scope Definition		Scope Verification
Time Management	Activity Definition Activity Sequencing		Schedule Control

[47] PMBOK, Chapter III, Mapping of Project Management Processes to the Process Groups and Knowledge Areas

THE BASICS OF CONSULTING PROCESS

	Planning	Executing	Controlling
	Activity Duration Estimation Schedule Development		
Cost Management	Resource Planning Cost Estimating Cost Budgeting		
Quality Management	Quality Planning	Quality Assurance	Quality Control
Human Resource Management	Organizational Planning Staff Acquisition	Team Development	
Communication Management	Communication Planning	Information Distribution	Performance Reporting
Risk Management	Risk Management Planning Risk Identification Qualitative Risk Analysis Quantitative Risk Analysis Risk Resource Planning		Risk Monitoring and Control
Procurement Management	Procurement Planning Solicitation Planning	Solicitation Source Selection Contract Administration	

3. FOUNDATION SKILL

3.1 Change Management

The purpose of change management is to promote and enable the adoption of changes that may occur as the result of project delivery, and thereby support the achievement of project results and outcomes. According to PMBOK[48], change management is an important feature of project management and successful project delivery. The activities of change management within the project delivery model are essential for minimizing barriers to change and for ensuring rapid and effective implementation of project outcomes. A project manager should know who the owner is to drive the change and what should make them engage in all phases of the project lifecycle.

---

[48] PMBOK, Project Management Body Of Knowledge

Initializaing	• Identify need for change • Assess readiness for change • Delineate scope of change
Planning	• Define the change approach • Plan stakeholder engagement • Plan transition and integration
Executing	• Prepare organization for change • Mobilize stakeholders • Deliver project outputs
Monitoring & Controlling	• Transition output into business • Measure adoption and outcomes/benefits • Adjust plan to address discrepancies
Closing	• Lessons learned • Measure benefits and value

*Across whole phases;
- Ongoing communication, consultation and representation of stakeholders
- Continuous improvement

Initializing

It identifies the change management activities, and the project manager should be aware that change management needs to be included in the project charter and preliminary planning. The project sponsor should be informed that the project will feature change management expertise and deliverables throughout the project delivery lifecycle.

- Identify the need for change

  - The project manager should work closely with the change manager to ensure that the business case and project charter are fully understood. As a minimum, the change manager will need to review the business case and project charter to understand the need for change. This is a mandatory prerequisite for assessing the organization's readiness and for defining the scope of the change. The change manager will provide feedback on the content of the charter, for example, to ensure that the charter acknowledges the need to include change management efforts within the project.

- Assess readiness for change

  - The change manager will conduct an organization readiness assessment to assess the organization's capacity for change based on the change characteristics of the project, the organization's history of adapting to change, sponsor evaluation, identification of change agents and stakeholders, etc. Depending on the nature of the project, deliverables may include a formal readiness assessment, a gap analysis, and risk assessment, high-level change management and communication strategies, a sponsorship engagement model, and a change management organization. Deliverables may be used by the project team to communicate with project sponsors.

- Delineate the scope of change

    - The change manager will delineate the scope of change from the review of business cases. Factors such as the number of employees affected by the project, the impact on processes, and the need for process changes will need to be known to develop a coherent change management strategy in alignment with the implementation plan. The project manager should gather and provide all data points including the change readiness report to the change manager.

Planning

Planning is the strategic part of the project management cycle. Its final deliverable is the project management plan that sets the framework for the whole cycle of implementation. Organizational change is a process of transformation heading for the desired state. In the planning phase, the subjects of the change are operating within the current state.

At this point in the project, the sponsor needs to ensure that stakeholder requirements are well-defined and well-organized change management in the project plan. This section describes the planning activities with deliverables typically conducted by the change manager over the implementation process.

- Define the change strategy

    - It drives the direction of change upon the assessments compared with change objectives that have developed in the initiation phase. To decide the direction, a consultant should consider how stakeholders are aware of the change, how to make the stakeholder attend the training, and how to address the resistance to the change process because the change has a unique approach by business and organization. The approach also gives an idea when a client designs the structure of the change management organization and mobilizes the resources.

- Stakeholder engagement

    - Strong involvement by a stakeholder will make the initiatives implemented, and the stakeholder can be identified along with the value chain.
    - For instance, a multi-purpose branch brings a wide range of self-service to the visitor instead of a sales assistant. Customers should check in their appointment by themselves at the Kiosk or the app on their cellphone. Once the check-in is accepted, the service specialist picks up the vehicle and

sends a questionnaire before investigating the condition. Also, s/he sends evidence of troubles and asks for approval of vehicle ownership for the resolution. To make the new process work as designed, the visitor needs to check in by themselves with enough knowledge of the new process or assistance from the staff on site. For this case, we can classify visitors, servicemen, and assistants on site will be stakeholders in the change. Also, the back-office process is another stakeholder.

- The expectation to the stakeholder will be 1) commitment to the change, 2) accept the change, and 3) lead the implementation and deploy the change.
- In the implementation planning, a consultant typically discusses with a client to define the roles and responsibilities of stakeholders over the implementation phase.

- Plan deployment and transition

    - Each initiative has typically designed to address individual challenges separately, and each challenge is related to another challenge. Although a consultant concentrates on the details of initiatives while developing an opportunity, he needs to keep a bird eyes' view when he drafts an implementation plan.
    - Implementation means a series of activities such as executing the initiatives, deploying the changes,

addressing challenges, and stabilizing the transition.

Executing

The existing process is converted to a transitional state when the client executes the change within their organization. When a stakeholder gets impacted by the change, they will naturally be in a defensive or passive position. So, a different measure or threshold of performance criteria will be considered to promote self-motivated changes by the stakeholder.

During the execution, a consultant and the client need to keep monitoring the progress from several perspectives such as organizational capability, process readiness, technical platform, and communication. A balanced scorecard will bring a smooth transition with fewer efforts to address resistance.

For getting organizational capabilities, the client should allocate talents under fully delegated authority. Process and technology will be enablers to realize the changes, and the client keeps monitoring whether the process with technology has enough capabilities to run the change. Communication is a kind of protocol to moderate conflicts and drive change management by topic, and stakeholders.

- Change readiness

- The change manager keeps ensuring and maintaining the change readiness of the organization. Change awareness, process capabilities, issue escalation, and performance review are typical topics to assess whether execution is on track.
- If the readiness drops down below the threshold, change manager escalates the challenges to the steering committee and asks

- Deploy the changes

  - The initiative brings impact to every aspect of the organization upon its deployment. For instance, the change of storage bean location requires ongoing changes in the operation process of a warehouse. Optimizing the storage bean location makes business profitable per unit space, and the implementation requires alignment among pickup/shipment scheduling, rearrangement of handling unit, and work fluency of each tasker.
  - So, while deploying and implementing the change, the change manager keeps articulating those change enablers to accomplish the objectives. Typically, it has several tools such as performance review, stakeholder training, and troubleshooting session as examples. When the deviation is out of allowance, it should be escalated to the process owner or steering committee.

Monitoring and controlling

Upon the feedback from stakeholders and accomplishment for each target, a steering committee approves the change officially. The approved changes are finally activated as a standard process, criteria, policy, and baseline. If the feedback or accomplishment is below the threshold, a client verifies whether the hypothesis was appropriate to elaborate on the change.

A client wants to reduce aged inventories and increase sales simultaneously. They believe it will give better cash flow and improve working capital. A client has driven the promotion and asked the team to verify the accomplishment. Unfortunately, it has not brought sales growth, and the aged inventory has the same level as before. The process owner escalates the challenges with observations to the steering committee to get a decision for further deployment. The steering committee will have to decide whether they will keep deploying the implementation or retrofitting all the changes back to the previous. Or, they can ask the team to review and develop a supporting solution for improving the effectiveness of implementation.

- Measures and rewards the best practice

    - While the organization adopts and internalizes the change into the existing process, the change manager keeps measuring the accomplishment with gaps where adaptation is lacking. Although the steering committee has approved the changes, the operation should be reviewed and shared with all stakeholders in a regular cadence. Sometimes, rewards and compensation will make the stakeholders keep involved in the changes.

- The change manager will need to evaluate the achievement, assess the adoption rate of the change, and document the lessons learned to distribute. The best practice will be applied for education, change management, and As-Is review.

- Reflect or update the existing performance measure

  - The new process or operation model will have a performance indicator, and a client revises the threshold with a target for each measure. Also, the compensation scheme will be revisited and aligned with the change.
  - At a company or business unit, the measure is reflected in MBO[49]. For an employee, it will be applied to the promotion and incentive model. If the change is associated with customer, vendor, or partner, it will be reflected in the terms and conditions of a contract with the party respectively. Premium discount or customer mileage is one of example.

---

[49] MBO, Management by Objective

Closing

Once the change is transferred to each business owner, the change manager prepares to close the project. Although all the operation is now each business's responsibility, the below items should be executed in regular cadence.

- Ongoing communication with stakeholders in internal/external to get feedback
- Regular assessment by an independent party
- Stakeholder awareness test in a regular cycle
- Regular report-out sessions to the steering committee
- Assessments and actions for continuous improvement

3.2 Communication

The importance of communication should be emphasized throughout the whole project phase. For instance, ineffective communication may bring a lack of involvement with misunderstanding in the implementation. Inadequately defined scope or unclearly designed task may cause it to fail. So, a project manager needs to gather ideas, explain the objectives of changes, and make stakeholders motivating by themselves. It is a typical generic part of communication.

BG Zulch has summarized the value of communication as a project manager below[50].

> "Managing a project requires constant selling and reselling of ideas, explaining the scope and methodologies of the project to diverse groups of people, threatening or bargaining with service providers and suppliers, or negotiating to settle disputes or interpersonal conflict between project team members or other stakeholders."

Typically, a project manager has a wide range of roles and responsibilities, and communication is one of the tasks to promote active engagement for the change over the project. A

---

[50] BG Zulch, "Communication: The foundation of project management", Procedia Technology 16 (2014), pp 1000 – 1009

project manager typically shares the progress, gathers feedback from stakeholders, escalates concerns to a steering committee, and moderates risks. If the communication has not been elaborated appropriately with the stakeholders, a client will experience redundant effort, rumors brought by misunderstanding, or compromised changes comparing what was originally intended.

Unless the stakeholder has the same awareness of the change, the project will be hard to accomplish the objective defined in the project charter.

"Communication is the most important aspect of project management because what project managers do the majority of the time is to communicate and coordinate efforts. To coordinate efforts, they have to gather a lot of information and deploy it across all organizations involved with the project."[51]

Types of communication in project management

Below tells several different perspectives of communication in project management.

- Project Perspective

    - For the project team, communication is elaborated into two domains such as internal and external

---

[51] Sarmann Kennedy, Northeastern University

communication.

- Communication for an internal team is usually working to promote the exchange of information between individuals who are actively working on a project. So, the purpose of communication is to improve cross-process integration.

  - For instance, company 123 wants to provide more selection of parts kits to increase sales and reduce inventory. Although, a package kit strategy for bundled parts offering requires collaboration across functions. In most cases, a parts master manager does not work closely with a pricing master manager to simulate price profitability. A project manager needs to encourage both process owners to work together for making new processes and criteria to prevent any side impact or adverse selection.

- On the other hand, communication for external parties is working to expedite progress sharing between the project team and key stakeholders not directly a part of the project. The changes in process or criteria will require active support from external parties such as customers, vendors, and partners. It is an important task to make them sit on the same page with internal stakeholders. As external communication is elaborated toward stakeholders who are not directly working on a project, it is often more formal protocol compared to internal communications.

- For instance, company 456 decides to run their inventory at vendors' locations, and they expect to improve space utilization within their facility. To realize the change, each vendor needs to create a location area with master data in their application system. Also, the vendor needs to maintain the inventory by status aligned with the production planning of company 456. To execute the change, a project manager keeps delivering the change direction with required actions as well as compensations when the vendor aligns it. Finally, the protocol will be listed on their procurement contract as official terms and conditions.

- Organizational Perspective

   - For a company, the communication will be categorized into three groups such as vertical, horizontal, and diagonal communication.
      - Vertical communication takes place between individual who operates on a different hierarchical level within the organization, and it has two types of communication such as "upward" or "downward" for the stakeholder. Upward communication means 1) the

project team escalates a particular roadblock that is getting in the way of completing a task to the project manager, or 2) asking the project manager to communicate with their superior on the progression of the project. Downward communication works in other directions, such as when the project manager assigns tasks to their team staff.

- Horizontal communication is working between individuals who operate on the same level within an organization. It's the communication that occurs between peers and colleagues, such as when a team has a regular standup call in the morning before they assemble items. Typically, they discuss the perception of defects with solutions, and it is a useful toolkit when a company looks for continuous improvement by six sigma.
- Diagonal communication is usually done across business functions or another business unit. For example, a field service agent needs to work with the procurement team for developing quality solutions.

- When engaging in vertical, horizontal, or diagonal communication, the project manager or team understands the underlying interests and uses that knowledge to frame their discussions.

- The Formality Perspective

  - This perspective is divided into two types such as informal and formal communication upon the degree of formality when a project manager elaborates on communication regardless of internal or external stakeholders.
  - Informal communications are often synonymous with internal communications outlined above. Daily emails, touch base, and unplanned meetings form the bulk of this communication, which is generally raw and unpolished. On the other hand, formal communication is seen as a product to be consumed. Reports, press releases, letters, public hearings, town hall meetings, and presentations to key stakeholders often fall into this bucket. Because of the audience that they are typically addressed to, these communications are often more highly produced and planned.

- Channel Perspective

  - The channel perspective refers to the channel or medium by which communication is transmitted or delivered. Common communication channels include verbal vs. non-verbal communication, in-person vs. remote or virtual communication, and written vs. oral communication. It's important to note that each communication channel offers benefits and disadvantages. The project manager should understand the benefits as well as the disadvantages and leverage them accordingly. In-person communication, for example, enables the parties to observe body language and gestures which might influence the message being sent, but it is not always possible due to the increasing use of remote teams in corporate environments. Similarly, written communication allows the writer to tailor their messaging to communicate precisely what they want to share, but it might lack certain subtleties that could otherwise be obvious in verbal communication. It's up to the project manager to understand which channel best applies to their unique requirements, and to balance those needs accordingly against the potential drawbacks of each channel.

Tips for effective communication in project

- Make use of technology

    - Just because your project team might be remote doesn't mean that all your communications should be done in written communication. A virtual meeting and collaboration technology facilitate face-to-face interactions. Recently, collaboration platform provides the same or similar experience as working offline by utilizing a virtual document room, video conferencing, group chat, recording, video clip library, tasks, minutes, an online survey, etc.

- Messaging solution may be a default protocol to send and receive communication, but the project manager needs to be aware of the limitation of email communication. Emailing is only communicating in one way, not both ways. A project manager needs to encourage more active communication or exchange among stakeholders instead of notifying the progress.

- Keep cultural and language barriers in mind

  - A company and organization are increasingly diverse, elevating the possibility that a member of your project team might not be a native English speaker. This might increase the risk of confusion during a project manager communicates about the changes. Being mindful of any cultural differences or language barriers of those involved in your team is, therefore, of critical importance. If necessary, a consultant utilizes an interpreter to promote more close communication without misunderstanding.
  - The other factor should be associated with cultural or behavioral challenges among stakeholders. For instance, some business units prefer to deploy the change by top-down communication when a client has grown up based on business acquisition rather than organic growth. Under the same condition, another business unit may prefer to decide and

promote the change based on bottom-up communication. Such as a language interpreter, a consultant needs to recommend client utilizes a change agent as an interpreter for the change.

- Understand who should get what information and how

  - A project manager is typically asked to play a quarterback for communicating the status over the project term across business functions. As the steering committee expects a project manager promotes information sharing among the stakeholders of a project, the project manager needs to moderate and drive productive communication against rumors or irrelevant information which might confuse them.
  - Usually, stakeholders are sensitive to anything related to their interests. It is not only their interest but also the organization's interest. Sometimes it is tightly related to their MBO metric. So, a project manager needs to consider impacts with a different position and develop mitigation to make the reactions ease when it comes. The mitigation will have different types according to the style of resistance, and it delivers like town hall meetings, open discussion, billboards, on-the-job training, education, role play, etc.
  - Communication is a toolkit to implement changes in the organization. However, it does not mean deploying the decision, and it should be a mutual exchange of perceptions for the common interest

based on the change initiative. To facilitate more open and transparent communication, a project manager needs to get advice from change agents and deliver a customized event to a specific stakeholder group if necessary.

ABOUT THE AUTHOR

JW SEOL has been worked as a consultant, IT leadership for global manufacturing companies based in Korea, India, China, and USA since 1994. His experiences are focused on IT strategy, technology adoption, business divestiture, and post merge and acquisition. He graduated from Korea Advanced Institute of Science and Technology with a Master of Science in management engineering. He lives in Atlanta, GA with his wife and 13 years old puppy.

MINHO CHO is a "Writer, Management Consultant, Pen Drawing Artist, PhD, MBA". He has been worked as a management consultant for 30 years, especially in Information Strategy Planning and Business Process Reengineering. Currently, he works as a pen drawing artist and illustrator in Seoul, Korea. Dr. Cho holds a PhD in digital management from TECH University of Korea and an MBA from University of Washington.

The authors have published below since 1999.
- The Basics of Consulting Process, US, 2022
- Introduction to Consulting, Seoul, Korea, 2006
- Consulting Practices, Seoul, Korea, 2002
- Consulting Process, Seoul, Korea, 1999

Made in the USA
Columbia, SC
26 November 2022

71841156R00104